Let's Go Skating

Let's Go Skating

Howard Bass

Stanley Paul
London

Stanley Paul & Co. Ltd
3 Fitzroy Square, London W1

An imprint of the Hutchinson Publishing Group

London Melbourne Sydney Auckland
Wellington Johannesburg Cape Town
and agencies throughout the world

First published 1974
© Howard Bass 1974
Drawings © Stanley Paul & Co. Ltd 1974

Set in Monotype Garamond
Printed in Great Britain by The Anchor Press Ltd,
and bound by Wm Brendon & Son Ltd,
both of Tiptree, Essex

ISBN 0 09 121050 X

A/796.9'1

Contents

It's a feeling of ice miles running under
your blades, the wind splitting open to
let you through, the earth whirling
around you at the touch of your toe, and
speed lifting you off the ice far from
all things that can hold you down.

SONJA HENIE

Illustrations

Acknowledgement for illustrations is due to London Lions Ice Hockey Club (10 and fig. 17), International Holiday on Ice Co. (6, 8, and 11), MK Skates Ltd (20), Tony Duffy (9, 13, and 17), Fred Dean and *Skate* magazine (1–5), and the Canadian Figure Skating Association (7, 12, 14 and 15).

1. Magic of the Ice

Skating still recalls to the older memory vivid thoughts of well-muffled, hardy athletes braving the winter elements, with the tougher, more rugged performer holding a clear advantage. How that situation has changed! Mechanically frozen indoor rinks in congenially heated buildings are now so accessible that many of the world's best exponents have reached championship class without ever skating outdoors. Even at wind-sheltered mountain resorts, where skating in the open air continues to be so healthfully rewarding, electrically refrigerated ice is often installed to ensure skating facilities in mild weather. Many such rinks have been built high in the Swiss Alps, a step once regarded as improbable as selling coffee to Brazil. Even in the hottest climes, skating now thrives where natural ice had never been seen. The sport is enjoyed by the Spanish in Madrid and Barcelona, by the Lebanese at Beirut and by South Africans in Johannesburg and Durban.

There are more than 1500 indoor rinks and an estimated five million skaters in the United States alone, figures which experts believe can be doubled within the next decade. Canada has over 800 figure skating clubs, with mushrooming memberships near 50 000 – the more dedicated enthusiasts, who represent only a small proportion of Canadians who skate.

The rate of expansion is roughly proportionate in most, but not all, of the thirty-two member nations of the International Skating Union, with every sign that the wave of worldwide popularity will go on rising. The trend is steadily transforming traditional ideas of pleasure-going, with demands for municipal ice rinks as loud as for swimming pools.

A regional survey in Britain has revealed that ice skating ranks third in national popularity among physical recreation activities in which men and women wish to take part. Yet recent progress in Britain has been slow in comparison with other European countries.

In France, for example, there are now more than 100 indoor rinks, including fifteen in the Paris area, the majority of them municipally owned. In Britain there are thirty-five – twenty in England (five in or near London), one in Wales and fourteen in Scotland. All at present are privately operated and most of the Scottish rinks are used primarily for curling. There are no British outdoor ice speed circuits, yet Holland has ten, all artifically frozen.

Unlike many other recreational amenities, a well-run civic skating rink can more than pay for its keep. It derives incomes from public sessions and education authorities, hire of boots and skates, sale of skates and allied equipment and clothing, skating instruction, specialized figure, dance, speed, hockey and curling clubs, varied catering and, where sufficient spectator accommodation is provided, galas, championships and competitions, special ice shows and hockey matches.

Very handsome profits are available for enterprising operators. Nowadays, many put a swimming pool and an ice rink in adjacent buildings, considerably reducing the overall running costs by designing a common power plant on a complementary basis.

Skaters come in all shapes and sizes, from all walks of life and in diverse kinds of physical condition. While the younger age groups form an expected majority, there are interesting examples of elderly enthusiasts who stay young in spirit and experience a feeling of wellbeing by pursuing a recreation which they find need not be strenuous. Lord Dowding, chief of the RAF Fighter Command during the Battle of Britain, said in his seventy-fifth year: 'At my age, skating is the perfect exercise because you can stop when you have had enough.' A treasured personal memory is of skating with Lady Astor on the outdoor Suvretta rink at St Moritz, Switzerland. She was 80 at the time and still revelled in the sport.

Very many skaters started as a direct result of medical advice. Children with physical weaknesses, with rickets, immature ankles and legs, even polio victims, have been successfully recommended by doctors to take up skating, often resulting in immeasurable benefit to their physical advancement.

Jacqueline du Bief, a French victim of wartime malnutrition, was told as a child that she could never skate. But she did and thereby improved her physique enough to become world champion in 1952.

A Londoner, Harry Whitton, has skated for years without any feet. After below-knee amputations in each leg, he attached skates to his artificial limbs and eventually passed a preliminary ice dance test. When showing me how he fitted the skates, Whitton acknowledged my concern about the risk with this shattering response: 'I have less to worry about than the others. If I fall, I have no ankles to break.'

In Canada, Margaret Deering has commendably succeeded with skating lessons for the blind. With her remarkable help, the South-West Vancouver Optimists Club and Jericho Hill School for the Blind have enabled more than a hundred unsighted children to learn elementary skating at the University of British Columbia's Thunderbird Arena.

Mrs Deering has found that, like most other skaters, her very special pupils derive improvement in their posture. She observed that blind children are often round-shouldered because normally they have no reason to look up. But the skates make it necessary for them to keep their backs erect.

Mitchel & King Skates Ltd, British makers of the world famous MK skates, sell more than a million blades a year in North America. Producing a range of precision models to satisfy the varying needs of figure, free, dance and hockey skaters, this company has invaded the United States and Canadian markets on an unprecedented scale. Champions were quickly attracted to their blades and popular demand followed their choice. For their outstanding export achievements, the manufacturers received the Queen's Award to Industry in 1974.

I am indebted to MK for their most helpful co-operation in the promotion of this book. In a manner of speaking, MK and I grew up together. Arthur Apfel, a masterly exponent of the cross-foot spin who came third in the 1947 World Figure Skating Championships, shortly afterwards showed me a blade he had designed and we arranged to discuss its merits with John Staples, the indefatigable MK founder and managing director. That blade put MK on its feet in more than one sense.

I was at the time a radio disc-jockey (though that term was not then in vogue), compèring broadcasts of music associated with skating stars of the day who were interviewed between each record.

The vital dependence on music has given skating an added dimension in comparison to other sports. Interpretation to the beat is all-important. Musical appreciation and skating technique thus developed so much in harmony that a star free-skater without a keen musical ear cannot really exist.

There is an irresistible magic, an apparently hypnotic magnetism which compels most skating first-timers to keep returning to a rink which seems to beckon like Shangri-La. Is it the music? Is it that glittering expanse of ice, an 'away from it all' atmosphere in complete contrast to life outside? Is it the happy comradeship that thrives among performers progressing together; the keen, invigorating air; a novel form of artistic self-expression? Or is it the sheer exhilaration from that smooth gliding movement which, some say, induces a thrilling sense of power in a temporarily different world? A combination of all these factors is probably the answer.

If this volume substantially enlightens readers about every branch of skating on ice, if it appreciably assists participants at all levels with technical descriptions and helpful comments, if it also entertainingly enthuses the sport's rinkside and television spectators – then the author's aim will be achieved.

2. How it All Began

One of the world's oldest sports, skating can be traced to the Stone Age. It probably originated in Northern Europe more than 3000 years ago. Mention of it was made in Scandinavian literature of the second century and, like skiing, it evolved from a primitive means of transport.

The first skates were made from shank or rib bones of the elk, ox, reindeer and other animals well before the discovery of iron, and there still exist in some of the world's museums bone skates believed to be at least twenty centuries old.

The oldest known skates were found bound to the skeleton of a Stone Age man in Friesland, Holland, made from a horse's cannon-bone during the second millennium BC. Those early skaters ground the bones down to make a flat surface and travelled with added propulsion from spiked poles.

In his *Description of London*, William Stephanides wrote in 1180: 'Some tie bones to their feet and under their heels; and shoving themselves by a little picked staff, do slide swiftly as a bird flieth in the air or an arrow out of a cross-bow.'

Skating has been popular on Dutch canals since the late Middle Ages, when speed skating began to evolve. A Dutch wood carving printed in 1498, early evidence of female participation, is the first known art-illustration of the sport. It depicts St Lydwina of Schiedam, who, in 1396 at the age of 16, fell and broke a rib while skating. She died in 1433 and later became known as the patron saint of skaters.

Wooden skates, because they were easier to shape, superseded

Figure 1. The accident to St Lydwina in 1396, when the patron saint of skaters broke a rib. This is the earliest known illustration concerned with skating, from a Dutch wood engraving printed in 1498.

bone before wood and metal combinations began to develop around the mid-1500s. An all-metal skate of sorts is supposed to have emanated from Russia in 1697.

Diarist Samuel Pepys described a sight he beheld on December 1, 1662, on the lake in St James's Park, London: 'Where first in my life, it being a great Frost, did see people sliding with their skeetes, which is a very pretty art.' Twenty-one years later, Pepys danced on the ice with Nell Gwynn.

Thirty years after the formation in Scotland of the world's first skating club, at Edinburgh in 1742, the first instructional book on skating was written by Captain Robert Jones and published in London in 1772.

Marie-Antoinette of France is reputed to have skated in Paris in 1776, when the sport became fashionable among the French aristocracy. General Napoleon, when a student at the École Militaire, narrowly escaped drowning in 1791 when skating on the fort moat at Auxerre.

The Skating Club of London was formed in 1842, not long before British servicemen introduced the sport to the United States and Canada. The first American club was founded in Philadelphia in 1849 and Benjamin West, a well-known painter, became one of the first American skaters of distinction.

In 1850, E. W. Bushnell of Philadelphia invented the first all-steel skate, which clipped on to the boot and dispensed with the previously tiresome use of straps. Blades were not commonly screwed on to the soles of the boots before the early 1900s.

In 1858, the first properly maintained rink was organized on the lake in New York's Central Park. The New York Skating Club was founded in 1860 and, two years later, it organized a skating carnival on the frozen Union Pond in Brooklyn.

The first Canadian rink opened at Toronto in 1868. By this time, a young American from Chicago had become the earliest really prominent skater with a truly theatrical flair. His name, now almost legendary in skating history, was Jackson Haines. Originally a professional ballroom dancer, with new ideas he developed a spectacular, revolutionary skating technique which at the time shocked the more conventionally minded.

After winning an American championship in New York, Haines went abroad in 1864 to electrify all Europe and instigated the Viennese school of skating, which contributed much to the present-day international style, following the formation of the Vienna club in 1867. 'To the American Skating King' were the words inscribed on Haines's tomb at Gamlakarleby, Finland, where he died in 1875.

Partly as a result of Haines's inspiration, serious skating thrived from 1880 in Scandinavia, where early great performers included Sweden's Ulrich Salchow, ten times winner of the world championship, and Norway's Axel Paulsen. Their names are still used today to describe the jumps which they created. From Scandinavia, too, other great names were to follow, not least among them Gilles Grafström of Sweden and Sonja Henie of Norway.

The first mechanically refrigerated rink was a small private one, the Glaciarium near King's Road, London, built by John Gamgee in 1876 with an ice surface measuring 40 by 24 feet (12 by 7.3 metres). It was, as the *London Illustrated News* records, constructed with galleries for the spectators, the walls being decorated with Swiss alpine and forest scenery painted by Durand of Paris.

A natural rink at Davos, Switzerland, was opened in 1877 and afterwards became an internationally recognized hub of the sport. The same year, an indoor rink opened in Manchester, England, and a chain reaction quickly followed on both sides of the Atlantic, prominent among the earliest covered ice stadiums being Baltimore, New York and Philadelphia, in the United States, Brighton and Southport in England, Brussels (Belgium), Paris (France) and Munich (Germany).

In 1879, the English and Scottish clubs united to form the sport's first federation, the National Skating Association of Great Britain. The United States Amateur Skating Association was inaugurated in 1886 and that of the Canadians in 1888. The International Skating Union, with headquarters at Davos, was instituted in 1892 and now has thirty-two member nations. Australia's first ice rink, the Melbourne Glaciarium, opened in 1904 and South Africa's at Johannesburg in 1909.

The ISU supervises both speed and figure skating – the latter including ice dancing. Officially recognized world speed championships date from 1893 and world figure championships from 1896. Figure skating gained Olympic status in 1908, followed by speed skating in 1924. This general summary of how it all began is supplemented by further historical details in the chapters concerned specifically with figure skating, ice dancing and speed skating.

3. The Essential Equipment

Boots, skates and skate guards are the sport's only essential specialized equipment. Skates and boots can be obtained either already fitted together as a set or, for the more discerning, separately. In the latter case, care should be taken to ensure that the person who screws the skates to the soles of the boots understands the exact positioning required. The staff in a rink skate-shop are naturally very experienced in this respect.

Sets can be hired for a nominal charge per session at public rinks. Although these cannot be expected to fit so well as one's own personal set, it is prudent to begin this way for the first half-dozen visits. If, after that, enthusiasm for the sport is sustained, the time is ripe for purchasing one's own equipment with every confidence that the cost is worthwhile.

Although often called a 'shoe', 'boot' is the more appropriate term for skating footwear because it covers the ankle. Normally made of black leather for men and white suède or nubuck for women, a good boot has a strong arch support reinforced with steel and a stiffening material around the heel and under the arch to prevent the foot from slipping to the side.

The fit of the boot is extremely important. It should be at least half a size smaller than normal footwear and fit tightly at heel, ankle and instep, but not round the toes. When fitting, women should wear only stockings and men light woollen socks because the boot must come to feel part of the foot. This it cannot do if a thick sock is worn. The latter can hinder proper circulation and can be surprisingly less warm than a thin sock.

B

If a new boot is fitted over silk or nylon stockings or tights, it can comfortably take an ankle sock or woollen stocking later.

For recreational skating, the 'figure' skate is the one to choose, readily distinguishable from a 'hockey' or 'speed' skate by its 'teeth' at the front of the blade. These teeth are known as a toe

Figure 2. The figure skating 'set' – with boot and blade screwed together.

rake or toe pick, of particular importance for spinning, which will not concern the beginner.

Hockey or speed skates are intended for those who specialize in these branches of the sport, and most rink managements frown upon, or even prohibit, their use during general public sessions, when unduly fast skating is discouraged for reasons of safety and comfort of others.

Unlike the straight hockey skate, the figure blade is slightly curved from heel to toe, usually set on a 7-foot radius. Very slightly longer than the length of the boot, the blade is about an eighth of an inch wide and its underneath is not flat, but has a hollow concave ridge along its length. This is termed 'hollow-ground'.

1079 1171

The sides of this hollow ridge are called 'edges', the edge nearer the inside of the foot being the inside edge, the other the outside edge. Nearly all correct, recognized movements on a figure skate are performed on one of its edges so that, whether

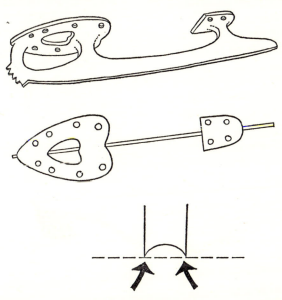

Figure 3. Three views of a figure skating blade. From the side (top) from above (centre) showing the screw-holes for fitting on to the sole of the boot, and from the front at ice level (bottom) showing that only the sides, i.e. edges of the blade, touch the ice.

in forward or backward direction, the skate is not flat but at an angle to the ice.

It is best to have the skate screwed to the boot so that the blade is fractionally nearer the inside of the foot rather than precisely down the centre of the sole and heel. Ideally, the blade should run underneath a point between the big toe and second toe.

The object of having the blade slightly inside the centre of the sole is to get the body weight more naturally over the skates. This feels more comfortably balanced, minimizing initial awkwardness and any illusion of weak ankles. If one's ankles are at all

A
796. 9'1

weak, skating in any case is the perfect exercise for strengthening them.

Boots and skates come in a wide range of prices. Something a little better than the cheapest should suit most beginners, whereas the expert, as in all sports, will go for the most expensive he can afford. The best boots are often tailor-made for championship-class performers and specialized blades for advanced skaters are enumerated in another chapter.

Stressing the importance of correct fitting and, therefore, the best quality one can afford, is not easy advice for parents whose children quickly grow out of one size and need another. Children progress so fast in this sport and sound equipment is so vital not only to assist improvement of their skating, but to avoid those adult deformities of the foot which so frequently originate from ill-fitting footwear during childhood.

This problem can best be met by parents getting together at rinks, bartering and exchanging their children's cast-off footwear while at the same time ensuring that good fittings in the right size are thereby obtained.

Good equipment is worth looking after. The blades will stay in good order only if reasonably protected when not actually skating. While wearing skates when not on the ice, it is most unwise to walk about without protecting the blades with wooden, rubber or plastic skate guards, which fit neatly over the blades and are available from any good sports outfitter.

At any skating competition, the participants can be observed peeling off skate guards just prior to going on the ice and putting them on again when leaving. Otherwise, the sharp edges can be quickly blunted.

Before putting the skates away, any slush should be wiped off. A few minutes should then be allowed for them to *warm* a little in the changing room. Cold skates, even after being wiped dry, will become moist again through condensation and so encourage rust on the all-important edges. Care should be taken not to dry the skates too near a radiator or fire because the changing extremes of temperature could possibly crack the blades or damage the boot leather.

After the skates are reasonably warm and dry, a little oil smeared

Figure 4. It is important to lace up properly. In the area immediately in front of the ankle, the laces should be pulled as close together as possible. Towards the top, slight slackness should allow the wearer to put a finger inside the top of the boot.

on the blades before slipping the guards on them will help to extend their duration of efficiency.

Skate blades need to be sharpened after about thirty hours' use. Experience and common sense will usually tell when they need it, but sometimes a poor ice surface can mislead a skater into believing the skates need sharpening before they do. At the other end of the scale are those newcomers who find themselves losing control because of blunt blades before anyone has told them skates have to be sharpened at all.

It is not good to sharpen blades more often than really needed, however, and the rink-shop expert should be consulted when in doubt. Experienced skaters are very wary about who sharpens their blades because it is a skilled job and it is a good idea to ask an experienced local skater to recommend a tried and trusted skate-grinder. Correctly ground blades are as vital to a figure skater as are properly tuned strings to a violinist, so a corresponding degree of loving care is natural.

Tips on lacing are listed in a later chapter. To minimize any possible loosening of hooks and eyelets, do not tug too sharply when lacing up the boots, nor bend down and pull upwards, but raise each foot to waist level and pull the laces towards the body rather than upwards. One should never walk about with any footwear unlaced, but with skating boots this is doubly important. Without the support of tightened boots, ankle injuries could result. There is also the risk of a blade cutting a dangling lace.

Boots will endure longer and more comfortably if fitted with trees or tightly stuffed newspaper each time before being put away. Thus they retain their shape better. Men's black leather boots can be well preserved by regular use of a suitable polish or cream. Women's white boots need white liquid non-spirit cleaners.

Is such painstaking effort worthwhile? Ask any top skater or leading performer in any other sport whether he prefers new footwear or a pair that have taken time and perseverance to become more comfortably moulded to the feet.

4. What Else to Wear

Recreational pleasure skating, as distinct from more serious competitive stuff, need not be an expensive hobby. The price of skates, boots and rink session charges are the only essential costs because one is not obliged to buy special clothing. It is instinctive to think of ice in terms of wrapping up well because this one had to do in the days of outdoor skating. Modern, well-heated indoor rinks, of course, now alter that.

Men and boys will find normal sports trousers and a shirt and sweater quite suitable. For women and girls, a slightly full skirt, or slacks, with a jumper are ideal. A pair of light woollen socks are recommended.

The more seasoned male performers may prefer special, tighter-fitting trousers and short, neatly cut jackets. The once conventional black is less favoured than it was and a bright coloured, close-fitting jacket with matching tights is very acceptable, with perhaps a badge on the breast pocket to give a smart finish.

Female wear through the years has changed in skating as much as in tennis. Pictures of performers in either sport during the 1920s show long narrow skirts extending well below the knees. How on earth they managed to perform well in such attire is difficult to imagine.

Until quite recent years, new skaters felt self-conscious in shorter skirts than those they wore outside the rink, but the miniskirt and hot pants fashions have since dispelled such qualms.

Equally suitable today for beginner and expert is a full, circular, pleated or gored skirt which flares from the hip line and is cut so that it falls several inches above the kneecap, and with matching, close-fitting panties. Woollen gloves are a useful accessory, not just to keep the hands warm, but to offer protection in a fall.

Bare legs without doubt look and feel fine for the so-called weaker sex when the temperature is high enough, but opera-length silk, nylon or woollen stockings or tights will keep the muscles warm and reduce the chances of rheumatic tendencies in later life. With or without stockings or tights, a pair of light ankle socks should always be worn.

Progressively more attractive skating clothes are to be found in the shops, some so *chic* that I am sure that the interest of many girls is first drawn to the sport because of them.

A general streamline effect while allowing full freedom of movement is the thought to bear in mind, with sufficient allowance across the shoulders to permit ease of arm movements. Headgear, if any, should be of the close-fitting, beret type. Otherwise, there is an obvious need to keep the hair securely tethered without using ordinary hairpins.

The more experienced female skater who contemplates practising figures will find it best not to wear too full a skirt that might billow out so that one's tracings cannot always be seen. For figure sessions, a plain and simple, freely fitting tailored dress is ideal, perhaps with a belted waist, long sleeves and several large pleats in the skirt to hold it down.

Attire for free-skating is something the new skater will learn by observation while progressing to the necessary technical standard to be able to free-skate. The women's dresses in this area are an entirely separate consideration, about as competitive as the skating contests themselves. Even the men have lately become far more inventive and enterprising in their choice of free-skating wear.

Although competition judges do not, or should not, directly mark for what the skater wears, they do mark for 'artistic impression' and that must be influenced, if only subconsciously, by smartness of appearance. Aside from this aspect, a free-skater is appearing before a public audience and so naturally wishes to look attractively and correctly dressed.

Men in the championship class now frequently select well-tailored, one-piece tight-suits in various colours, male pair and dance skaters usually matching the colours worn by their partners. Light tuxedo-style jackets with contrasting dark coloured trousers are also seen. All this is a great leap forward from not so far distant days when men were generally expected to sport all-black attire for free-skating.

For the girls, crêpe and other elastic materials have the advantage of retaining shape and allowing maximum freedom of movement so important in jumps and spins. Chiffon and lamé are also well favoured. Sequins and other decorative trimmings can further enhance the appearance and, needless to say, some of the costumes used in top-flight championships can be quite costly.

It may be helpful to note that, while lamé or satin may appreciably smarten the appearance of a slim girl, such shiny materials do tend to emphasize the plumper figure, as can 'fussy' ornamentation. Subtle detail in embroidery in any case cannot be appreciated at much distance, so more attention is perhaps better spent making sure that the cut of the costume shows off the figure to best effect.

The skater likely to be seen on television is advised to avoid black or white apparel or anything particularly dazzling. It may be worth remembering, too, that on a black-and-white screen red and blue transmit with a similar darkness density and are thus indistinguishable – as soccer viewers watching a blue-shirted team against red-shirted opponents know only too well.

A final tip when dressing for skating at any level. The appearance of expensive, immaculate clothes can be marred by soiled boots. If they should be white, do make sure that they are and – while inspecting them – double-check that the laces are properly tied and not frayed. A loose or broken lace while skating can cause a maddeningly unnecessary fall.

5. Basic Questions Answered

If you are a newcomer to ice skating, it is only natural that many questions must spring to mind concerning your newly chosen sport. You are probably very conscious of your lack of skill and may wonder how to learn as efficiently, speedily and inexpensively as possible.

Why should I learn to skate? Ice skating is a wonderful sport for family participation. All ages can have fun together and enjoy healthy socializing. The exercise uses all of the body muscles and improves blood circulation. You can put in as much effort and energy as you wish. You can learn at an early age and continue well into the later years. The sport develops co-ordination probably better than any other and gives poise, grace, rhythm and good posture. For young people it provides an ideal atmosphere for mixing, forming friendships and enjoying company under conditions of unrestrictive supervision.

What basic equipment do I need to begin? There are three types of ice skate. The most popular is the figure skate, which is designed for maximum manoeuvrability. Then there is the hockey skate, which gives limited manoeuvrability but greater speed, and finally there is the speed skate, designed exclusively for racing use.

If you wish to learn to skate purely for the fun of going fast or if you plan to join a hockey club, then your choice would be hockey skates. If you wish to learn to make turns, jumps and spins, then your choice will be figure skates. Skaters who rent their skates will see that most rinks use only figure blades for rental purposes.

You will probably want to rent your skates at first, but you will soon wish to have your own. Here are some useful tips to follow when deciding to buy:

1. Your boots should have two layers of leather in the uppers. The linings should be leather and not canvas.

2. The boots must have a strong ankle support, sometimes called a 'counter'.

3. The boots should be of top-grain leather with a sole rigid enough to retain the screws that hold the blade to the boot.

4. Your blades preferably should be fixed to the boots with screws since this will enable you to reset the blades if adjustment is needed to suit your own individual requirements.

5. The blade should be of high tempered steel, with the skating edge ground to a shallow concave producing two sharp edges throughout its entire length. The blades should be nickel or chrome plated.

6. Do not buy the most expensive blades unless you know how to use them. A 'good buy' is not necessarily costly. You can always consult the experienced rink staff.

Should I use the same size footwear for skating as for walking? You will seldom use the same size skating boot as your regular street shoe. Up to size 4 you will probably take a half-size smaller in skating boot. Above size 4 you will probably take a full size smaller. The exception to this rule concerns those people who have extremely wide feet, and they may expect to wear the same size as their regular street shoe. Remember, the more snug the fit, the better the support for your ankles.

Is there a special way to put on ice skates? Yes, you must be sure that the laces are really loose all the way down before you attempt to put the boot on, otherwise you may think the boot is too small when your foot is actually being restricted by the laces. Pull your socks up to remove any wrinkles. Once your foot is right in, pull the long tongue up firmly in case you have pushed it down in front of your toes. Pull your heel back in the boot as far as possible. If you have too much space in front of your toes, select a smaller boot.

To tie the laces, leave the bottom area relatively loose so that the toes are not cramped. Once past the lowest pair of eyeholes, tie the laces firmly until you reach the area of the ankle. Around the ankle you must tie very tightly. On most boots this area coincides with the top pair of eyeholes, and from this area upwards most boots are equipped with hooks. The bottom hooks should be tied tightly, and then you may go back to tying the lacing just firmly again. When you reach the top of the boot the lacing should be relatively loose, so that you can easily insert your finger between your sock and the boot. If you tie too tightly at the top, you may restrict circulation.

How do I take care of my skates?

1. Always keep your blades sharp and have them checked after every 15 skating sessions. Dull blades often cause errors in skating technique.

2. Use skate-guards when off the ice, to protect your blades and prevent injury to other skaters.

3. Never put skate-guards on until you have dried the blades.

4. Remove the skate-guards at home after skating to ensure perfect drying. The change in temperature between the ice rink and your home can cause condensation on the blades.

5. Keep boots clean by using a good quality cleaner which will not damage or dry out the leather. Most ice rinks supply these special cleaners.

6. An occasional coat with a heel and sole enamel prevents water from separating the heel and outer sole layers, and will prevent rotting.

What kind of skating outfit should I wear? For men and boys, slacks, shirt and sweater are ideal. Ladies and girls usually wear slacks and sweaters as beginners, but later graduate to more sophisticated skating styles such as suntan coloured tights over panties, then trunks to tone with the skating skirt over the tights. Skirts are worn very short, so that when the skater is standing upright the hem of the skirt just hides the trunks. Ladies should control their hair without hairpins as these may drop on the ice and cause an accident. It is a good idea to wear gloves as over 90 per cent of all skating accidents consist of minor cuts to the fingers.

Should I take skating lessons? It is always a very good idea to take skating lessons. You will be surprised at your rate of learning.

Even if at first you cling to the handrail, unable to take a step, you will usually find that you will get along quite well after only one lesson.

Group lessons are available at most ice rinks. It is generally not a good idea for adults to share a lesson with children. The instructor will use different teaching techniques with the various age groups, and while adults can understand analysis and logic, children will more often respond to a more emotional approach to the teaching.

Can I practise figure skating by myself? Yes. Many ice rinks organize special skating periods open only to figure skaters, and each skater is given a private area on the ice in the shape of a rectangle, approximately 18 feet wide and 40 feet long. This area is known as a 'patch'. You need perfectly clean ice to show every mark that is imposed by the blades.

6. Choosing the Best Blades

Why are there so many different kinds of blades? The part of a skate that matters most is the blade. Its thickness, contour and toe pick design determine how effectively a skater can perform. There are marked variations to suit a skater's particular wishes. For example, speed skating calls for especially thin blades which have a long ice lay and are therefore nearly flat. Hockey blades must be fast but a little thicker for added ruggedness. Also, a hockey blade has around a 9-foot radius contour which gives less ice lay, enabling some degree of manoeuvrability.

Maximum manoeuvrability is required for the figure blades and the contour has the shortest ice contact with nearer 7-foot radius. To assist with jumps and spins the figure blade needs toe picks, whereas both hockey and speed skates are smoothly curved at the toe.

When I am no longer a beginner, to which blades should I change? As a beginner, you have probably rented your skates. Most rentals use figure blades and the Rinkmaster is the world's most popular rental. You will now know whether you prefer speed, hockey or pleasure skating.

For speed or hockey, you will choose the special blades available. This book caters mainly for the pleasure and figure skating interests. An ideal inexpensive blade for pleasure is the Ice Time. These blades are hardened and tempered, have a smooth ground skating edge and are attractively finished in polished chrome over heavy nickel.

I want to become an expert figure skater. Which blades are for me?
You will need well-made blades of advanced design. The Single
Star is ideal for commencing. It has large toe picks to assist with
jumps. The hollow ground edge is polished to give smooth
skating. As you progress, the Professional blade has even larger
picks and is more ruggedly built to withstand the most rigorous
free-skating. It is precision hollow ground, providing uniform
height edges free from 'flats' that prevent smooth controlled
skating.

I want to be a champion! Unless you are truly dedicated, do not
try. If dedicated, then a range of competition models is available
to meet all that a figure champion can demand. The most popular
is the Phantom, a blade designed to enable advanced skaters to
excel in all forms of figure skating without moving to the
specialist models.

The toe picks are ideal for advanced free skating but are not
positioned too low to impair figures. The blade is side-honed,
both to reduce weight and, more important, to give a better blade
edge. Side-honing increases ice grip at pronounced angles where
most needed. Well balanced, superbly finished and precision
hollow ground, you will always take a pride in your Phantoms.

What are the competition specialist blades? Specialist areas are the
figure, free and ice dancing. Blades are designed for each of these.
For competition use, skaters will generally keep separate blades
for different purposes.

Why is a figure blade different? In order to perform high-quality
compulsory figure tracings, the blade must possess a shallow
precision hollow grind in order to minimize the problem of
double-tracking. The toe picks must be a little higher, in order to
avoid catching on loops and spoiling clean ice tracing. The world
famous Gold Test blade meets these requirements and is used by
champions everywhere.

What about free-skating? It is in free-skating that an individual
displays athletic and artistic prowess. Jumps, spins and combination movements thrill performer and audience alike. As in many
other sports, progressive achievement is a feature of free-skating.
Jumps have become more spectacular, spins faster. These are
made possible by improved techniques and refined equipment.

The Gold Star blade has been designed to meet everything a brilliant free-skater can demand of skates. Toe picks are large, in combination form and include one large high pick – affording a skater really good ice grip when taking off in jumps. There is an extra deep hollow grind to prevent slipping, and the blade is side honed to give maximum grip along its edge. The whole skate is powerful and rugged, yet exceptionally light in weight, obtained by meticulous balance and removal of all unnecessary steel.

Do I need different blades for ice dancing? Only the really competent ice dancer will need the special blades obtainable. The competition Dance model embodies all features required for peak performances. The blade heel is specially shortened to avoid skates colliding during fast and intricate overlap footwork. The skating edge is fined down to hockey-blade width, to facilitate high-speed movements for minimum effort.

All the blades mentioned and illustrated, readily obtainable throughout the world, are made by MK Skates, the respected specialists in this field. Their assistance is acknowledged in respect of the foregoing technical information.

7. The First Strokes

Go to an ice rink and just watch for a while. See how others perform. Feel the atmosphere. After a time you will sense the friendliness and enjoyment around you. Any nervousness about attempting the unknown will soon vanish, and you will want to try it for yourself.

Beginners may find the first visit a little awe-inspiring. How wonderful it would be to go straight out to the centre of the rink and skid to an impressive halt amid a spectacular shower of ice flakes – just like the skating stars of television!

Seeing the comical antics of other first-timers striving to remain upright with one hand on the barrier rail can easily cause one to hesitate before 'looking like a fool' in public.

To offset this self-consciousness and speed up early progress, it is a good idea during your first appearance on ice to engage the personal service of a junior instructor. His or her help for twenty minutes is well worth the small cost at this point, because you stand to gain confidence and a sense of balance more quickly. Then, during your second visit, without such help you may well find yourself able to skate unaided to the centre of the rink.

An instructor during the first visit can undoubtedly accelerate early progress. Alternatively, or additionally, you can seek the helping hand of some friendly-looking skater, who may happily steer you around. Reasonable but slower progress without anyone's help can be made by holding on to the barrier rail, which normally goes all the way round the rink.

When it comes to it, there is usually a generous spirit of

c

comradeship among fellow beginners and very soon you are sure to find yourself being assisted cheerfully and, not much later, helping others, and winning new friends in the process.

Your feet will at first want to run away from you, so very small steps should be taken at the beginning. You will be concerned about falling, but there is no need to be. In fact, the sooner it happens the better, because you will realize that it is not nearly so bad after all, and some falls are inevitable in the process of learning. Also, everyone else will be so preoccupied with their own progress that little or no attention is likely to be paid to the most inelegant capers, probably no less dignified and very similar to those once experienced by every eventual champion.

Falling is not nearly so bad as you might have supposed, but you can make it even less fearsome by relaxing the muscles and not stiffening up when you feel yourself going. Gloves will protect your hands whenever they touch the ice.

Skating forwards

Having progressed in small steps for a short while, it soon becomes possible to stand without grabbing the barrier rail so often, and you can now try skating forwards properly.

To begin this exercise, stand with the feet parallel and about twelve inches apart, with knees slightly bent. Now, for the first stroke, turn the left foot out to an angle of forty-five degrees, at the same time turning the ankle slightly inwards so that the *inside* edge of the left blade can be felt making contact with the ice.

With weight on the left foot and knees slightly bent, push forward on to the right foot, transferring the weight on to it. With the ankle kept as upright as possible, a forward gliding movement will be experienced on the right skate.

Keeping the body erect as the right foot glides forward, lift the left foot just clear of the skating surface and bring it up beside the right; then, for the second stroke, turn the right foot out to an angle of forty-five degrees, turning the ankle in enough to feel the inside edge, and now push on to the left foot, transferring the weight on to it, at the same time being conscious that the left

*Figure 5. The starting position. Put the right foot behind the left in
'T'-formation. The right foot gives a push to help the forward movement
with the left.*

shoulder goes well to the left in doing so. The starting position
is illustrated.

So the process continues. Remember to keep the body upright,
and try to look straight ahead and not at your feet. As confidence
and ability improve with each stroke – as the stride is called in
skating – you can gradually lengthen them. Eventually, try feeling
the strike forward on the outside edge of the blade rather than
on the flat.

Always push forward on the whole skate, and never on the
toe-point. You will gradually be able to lean the left shoulder
farther over to the left while skating forwards with the left foot,
and the right shoulder farther over to the right while skating
forwards with the right foot. This feeling brings an added

confidence and sense of balance comparable to that of riding a bicycle.

The left-foot-forward movement should take you in a slight left-hand curve, and the right-foot-forward movement in a right-hand curve. Do not, in fact, try to skate in a straight line,

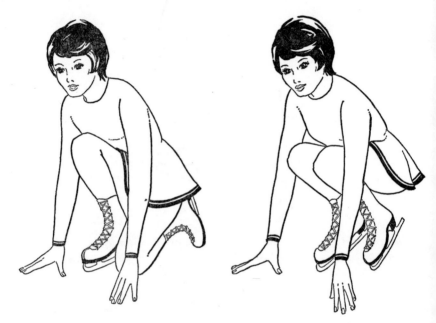

Figure 6. When falling, do not try to get up too quickly. First kneel on one knee. Then, with feet together and with pressure on the toe-rakes of the skates, push up by pressing the hands on the ice.

but veer first to the left and then to the right with alternate strokes. Remember to bend the knees well at the start of each stroke.

Memorize the following most common errors. Resist the impulse to walk; think in terms of gliding. Do not attempt to push with the toe of the blade, as this will cause you to fall forwards. Avoid waving the arms like propellers; hold them steadily, about waist-high, palms downwards.

Do not look down at the feet because this upsets the balance. Instead, hold the head erect and look straight ahead. Relax when falling, avoiding the temptation to grab wildly at anything or anybody to prevent it. Do not hurry to get up again, but stay calm and kneel first on one knee, push on to the ice with both hands and, with skates close together in 'V'-formation, rise slowly.

Braking

It is easy to be carried away by early enthusiasm and to develop the ability to skate fast before learning how to stop safely. I realize now my folly in learning to skate forwards and backwards at a pretty fair pace without having a clue about braking. For your safety and everyone else's, learn how to brake as soon as possible so that you can feel capable of coping with any emergency – like avoiding someone who may suddenly fall in your path.

The simplest method of braking when skating forwards is to drag the inside skate-blade of the free leg lightly on the ice behind the skating foot, at the same time keeping the weight forward over the skating foot. As the blade touches the ice, snowy flakes gather in front of the blade, helping the slowing-up process, and you finish with the feet in a 'T'-formation, the heel of the front foot just in front of, and almost touching, the inside middle of the skating foot.

Another elementary way is to put the heel of the free skate on the ice in front of the skating foot. Either way, do it gently without jerking.

There are various methods of more advanced and effective 'skid' stops, such as turning both feet sideways and skidding with the weight pressed against the sides of the skates, but it is not advisable to try this way until first becoming a competent mover forwards and backwards.

Ask a fellow learner or, better still, a more experienced skater, to watch while you learn how to brake, and so avoid a few unnecessary falls. As soon as you know how to brake safely, you can skate forwards more quickly and try gliding for longer periods on each foot. All this before you attempt to skate backwards.

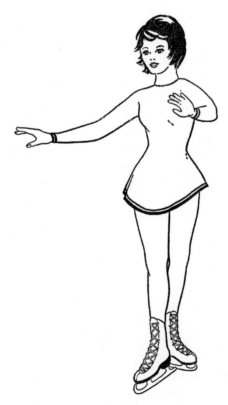

Figure 7. Learning to brake before skating fast will increase early confidence and control, so first perfect the 'T'-stop, paying special attention to the foot positions.

Skating backwards

In half a dozen sessions it is quite possible to become, through sheer practice, sufficiently skilled in forward skating round the rink to be anxious to learn a variation, and the natural sequel is skating backwards.

Stand with toes pointed in and heels out. Then, bending the knees, push from the inside of the left blade on to the right foot, and raise the left leg just clear of the ice, travelling backwards on bent knee and slowly straightening it as the free leg is brought to the side of the right foot. Strike off each step slowly, and bring the feet together again before making each new stroke.

You must not lean forwards when skating backwards. You should keep your head, shoulders and hips over the ball of the skating foot. Your knees must not be kept straight, but must bend readily as you glide backwards, then straighten gradually as you bring your trailing foot up to the side of the other before again bending the knees to start another backwards stroke.

Do not take the weight of your body off the foot which is doing the skating. Where the weight is the action happens and, the more you become conscious of this, the more you will feel it is the correct positioning of your weight which is mainly causing your feet to move where you want them to go.

As soon as you are balancing well enough to have time to concentrate more on style, avoid turning up your free foot too much. The more you point it, the more elegant your movements will look to others. When skating backwards, do not look down or where you have come from, but look over your shoulder in the direction you want to go.

8. All on Edge

Having learned basically to skate forwards and backwards, and to brake comfortably, it is time to become more conscious of the importance of the fact that the ice figure skate is hollow-ground, each skating blade having two edges which run the length of the skate, the inside edge and the outside edge. From now on, you should think in terms of skating on a particular edge, and that there are thus only four moves on either foot:

1. Forward on the outside edge.
2. Forward on the inside edge.
3. Backward on the outside edge.
4. Backward on the inside edge.

Every skating figure is based on those four movements. Each simple movement on an edge should be taken individually on its own merit, no matter how complex the complete figure to which it contributes. Skating on an edge entails a leaning of the body over that edge sufficient to cause a forward or backward movement in a curve. This curve, when continued, will describe a circle.

It may help your early sense of balance now to think of a cyclist's lean as he turns a gentle corner. The lean is proportionately greater according to the speed and angle of the turn or curve, and just as a cyclist leans over *with* the cycle, so a skater should lean over *with* the edge of the blade he is using. Smoothness without jerking throughout any skating movement is the aim, and the only way to achieve that is by patient practice and repetition.

1. Dorothy Hamill, United States runner-up in the 1974 world championships.

2. Alexander Gorshkov and Ludmila Pakhomova, Russian world ice dance champions a record five times, 1970–4.

3. John Curry, Britain's European bronze medallist in 1974.

4. Janet Lynn, United States runner-up in the 1973 world championships.

Experiment by skating consciously on inside edges, then on outside edges. Lengthen strokes as confidence grows. Lean farther over and forward while keeping the weight on the skating foot.

Bend the skating knee freely. Keep the non-skating foot pointed as elegantly as possible. Hold the arms out about waist-high to balance, palms downward. Hold them steadily, and do not wave them backwards and forwards as when walking. Keep each stroke smooth and deliberate, without jerking.

Cultivate a sense of rhythmic movement by timing the strokes to the rinkside loudspeaker music. When there is no music, hum a tune – try the 'Skater's Waltz' – and time the strokes to it. Never hesitate to get a friend to watch and comment. He can see faults in style which you cannot.

Figuring it out

You may have ambitions to take proficiency tests and win medals for passing them. You may want to enter competitions and championships. You may be more concerned with the social pleasures of dancing on ice. You may have set your sights on eventually joining a professional ice show. Or you may be interested solely in the pleasure of skating purely for fun, and as a healthy recreation.

Whichever reason you have in mind, to enjoy any kind of skating success you need at first to study the art of 'school' figure skating, the so-called compulsory figures, a knowledge of which provides a sound basis for better progress in every type of skating.

You can improve in an interesting way by taking tests, very simple ones at first, and progressively winning a bronze, silver and, eventually perhaps, even the coveted gold medal.

The internationally recognized schedules of compulsory figures in ice skating are listed, and illustrated by diagrams, at the end of this chapter. Most of them must be skated first on the right, and then on the left foot. Each figure is started from a stationary 'rest' position, and is composed of a set pattern in the form of either a two-lobe or three-lobe 'eight'. In tests and competitions, each figure or pattern is skated three times.

Specialized tuition from an instructor will be necessary if you advance seriously in this way. Occasional twenty-minute or half-hour lessons for moderate performers need not be unduly expensive, but coaching for the more advanced grades naturally costs more.

This applies more to the senior championship hopefuls. To take proficiency medal tests, you first have to become a member of your national skating association, under whose authority the tests are organized and judged.

Do you just want to skate around at the rink without bothering to improve technique very much? Or are you ambitious enough to want to skate reasonably well? Either way, you will progress better by practising at least the most elementary of the figures. Ask a more experienced skater to help you learn them. There is usually someone in the centre of the ice practising figures, and such enthusiasts are often very happy to lend a helping hand. Better still, you can first take a lesson or two with an instructor and then practise the way you have been shown. Instead of seeking individual instruction, you can join group tuition classes, which work out cheaper. Details are available at your rink.

Quite soon, you should be good enough to skate a preliminary test, which is not very difficult and does not need much experience. To do this, you must first become a member of your national skating association. Or you can join the skating club at your rink and through it get lots of friendly advice and become an affiliated member of the national association.

Association members receive each year a copy of its official handbook and other books which contain full details of figures, tests and championships.

Compulsory figures

When describing the forty-one internationally recognized compulsory skating figures, the abbreviations which follow are commonly used. Learning the first and most elementary of these

figures is strongly recommended if you wish to progress seriously
beyond the beginner's recreative pleasure stage.

R = right	b = backwards	T = three	RK = rocker
L = left	o = outside	LP = loop	C = counter
f = forwards	i = inside	B = bracket	

Figure	No.	Description	Marks factor of value

Curve eight

1. Rfo—Lfo		1
2. Rfi—Lfi		1
3. Rbo—Lbo		2
4. Rbi—Lbi		2

1

Change

5a. Rfoi—Lfio		1
b. Lfoi—Rfio		1
6a. Rboi—Lbio		3
b. Lboi—Rbio		3

5a

Three

7. RfoTbi—LfoTbi		2
8a. RfoTbi—LbiTfo		2
b. LfoTbi—RbiTfo		2
9a. RfiTbo—LboTfi		2
b. LfiTbo—RboTfi		2

7

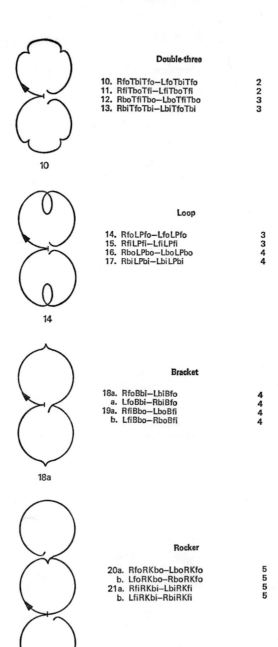

Double-three

10. RfoTbiTfo—LfoTbiTfo	2
11. RfiTboTfi—LfiTboTfi	2
12. RboTfiTbo—LboTfiTbo	3
13. RbiTfoTbi—LbiTfoTbi	3

10

Loop

14. RfoLPfo—LfoLPfo	3
15. RfiLPfi—LfiLPfi	3
16. RboLPbo—LboLPbo	4
17. RbiLPbi—LbiLPbi	4

14

Bracket

18a. RfoBbi—LbiBfo	4
a. LfoBbi—RbiBfo	4
19a. RfiBbo—LboBfi	4
b. LfiBbo—RboBfi	4

18a

Rocker

20a. RfoRKbo—LboRKfo	5
b. LfoRKbo—RboRKfo	5
21a. RfiRKbi—LbiRKfi	5
b. LfiRKbi—RbiRKfi	5

20a

22a

Counter

22a.	RfoCbo—LboCfo	4
b.	LfoCbo—RboCfo	4
23a.	RfiCbi—LbiCfi	4
b.	LfiCbi—RbiCfi	4

24a

One foot eight

24a.	Rfoi—Lfio	3
b.	Lfoi—Rfio	3
25a.	Rboi—Lbio	4
b.	Lboi—Rbio	4

26a

Change three

26a.	RfoiTbo—LboiTfo	3
b.	LfoiTbo—RboiTfo	3
27a.	RfioTbi—LboiTfi	3
b.	LfioTbi—RbioTfi	3

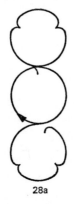

28a

Change - double three

28a.	RfoiTboTfi—LfioTbiTfo	3
b.	LfoiTboTfi—RfioTbiTfo	3
29a.	RboiTfoTbi—LbioTfiTbo	4
b.	LboiTfoTbi—RbioTfiTbo	4

30a

Change - loop

30a.	RfoiLPfi—LfioLPfo	4
b	LfoiLPfi—RfioLPfo	4
31a.	RboiLPbi—LbioLPbo	6
b.	LboiLPbi—RbioLPbo	6

32a

Change - bracket

32a.	RfoiBbo—LboiBfo	5
b.	LfoiBbo—RboiBfo	5
33a.	RfioBbi—LbioBfi	5
b.	LfioBbi—RbioBfi	5

34a

Paragraph three
(three - change - three)

34a.	RfoTbioTfi—LfiTboiTfo	4
b.	LfoTbioTfi—RfiTboiTfo	4
35a.	RboTfioTbi—LbiTfoiTbo	4
b.	LboTfioTbi—RbiTfoiTbo	4

36a

Paragraph double three
(double three - change - double three)

36a.	RfoTbiTfoiTboTfi—LfiTboTfioTbiTfo	5
b.	LfoTbiTfoiTboTfi—RfiTboTfioTbitfo	5
37a.	RboTfiTboiTfoTbi—	
	LbiTfoTbioTfiTbo	6
b.	LboTfiTboiTfoTbi—	
	RbiTfoTbioTfiTbo	6

38a

Paragraph loop
(loop - change - loop)

38a.	RfoLPfoiLPfi—LfiLPfioLPfo	6
b.	LfoLPfoiLPfi—RfiLPfioLPfo	6
39a.	RboLPboiLpbi—LbiLPbioLPbo	6
b.	LboLPboiLPBi—RbiLPbioLPbo	6

40a

Paragraph bracket
(bracket - change - bracket)

40a.	RfoRbioBfi—LfiBboiBfo	6
b.	LfoBbioBfi—RfiBboiBfo	6
41a.	RboBrioBbi—LbiBfoiBbo	6
b.	LboBfioBbi—RbiBfoiBbo	6

9. Starting to Free-skate

Most people gain the greatest pleasure from free-skating. Some methodical execution of at least the easiest of the school figures is necessary before you can be technically capable to free-skate with success. Free-skating means that the performer is in no way restricted in what he attempts, how he performs or in what sequence. Free-skating is what we see in skating shows, in skating exhibitions and as the more spectacular part of a figure skating championship.

In competition, your freedom is influenced by the need to incorporate, according to the technical standard involved, as many difficult movements as possible within the few minutes allotted, in order to gain the highest possible marks. These are awarded:

1. For technical merit, difficulty of achievement and order of sequence being of prime concern.
2. For artistic impression.

In non-competitive exhibitions or theatrical skating displays, the natural tendency is to do what looks spectacular, irrespective of technical finesse or difficulty. Only the best performer *looks* free, many looking too tense, studious and conscious of the occasion.

Spiral movements

The first thing to learn in the natural sequence of free-skating movements is a spiral or 'run' – the holding of an edge at ap-

Figure 9. This basic position, and the one on page 50, show typical spirals with hands outstretched for effect and to help the balance.

preciable speed with an exaggeratedly posed position. Impatient though you may be to improve, it would be putting the cart before the horse to attempt exciting-looking spins or jumps before learning how to glide steadily with a confident, even flow. Without this ability, anything more advanced will look awkward or disjointed.

The jumps and spins will come more naturally and easily after you have graduated through the simple spirals and linking steps. Artistic impression is as important as technical merit, and the exciting thing about free-skating is that there is no limit to what may be attempted or created. The scope is infinite, allowing a

D

Figure 10. Note how the toe of the free boot shown here (and in the other illustrations in this chapter) is pointed outwards as far as possible.

freedom of expression that becomes more exhilarating and satisfying as your musical appreciation and sense of showmanship increases.

Moving statues

The quickest visual picture of spirals lies in their apt description as 'moving statues'. Indeed, ideas for good, effective spirals may well be improved by the study of some of the most graceful poses in sculpture and painting. Just as some of these depict feminine grace, so do others imply masculine strength and speed. Positions chosen must depend on your build and ability.

Figure 11. A spiral with hands in front. From this position the arms and hands can be slowly and gracefully opened outwards while gliding forwards.

Holding the position while gliding unwaveringly is the hall-mark of a good spiral. The ability to control spirals, either forwards or backwards, provides the basis of a free-skating repertoire, to which jumps and spins may be added gradually.

Having painstakingly traced some figures on the ice, spirals will come quite easily to you, and now you will feel free to devise your own variations and positions of spirals which best suit your shape and height. You must control and hold various 'moving statue' positions, forwards and backwards, then join them together with suitable linking steps. Then you will have the groundwork for adding jumps and spins. Some typical spiral positions are shown.

10. The Art of Jumping

Each successive generation of skaters is jumping better and higher than the last as new knowledge and practice of technique advances. The art depends very much on the strength of spring, as well as timing the take-off, which is why boys tend to be higher and more powerful jumpers than girls. All initial effort should be concentrated on height. Project forward and up first, *then* rotate.

How to rotate

The act of rotating is normally started by pulling the arms inwards to the body. Most skaters find that they rotate more naturally one way than the other. As soon as it is realized which way comes more easily, use it for all your jumps and spins.

Numerous elementary toe-point jumps, easy to accomplish and pleasing to the eye, include the bunny hop, mazurka jump and ballet hop. All of these are made gracefully effective by extending the free leg well out before putting the toe-point down, remembering that the spring comes mainly from the skating leg and *not* the toe-point. These simple jumps do not require advanced technical knowledge, and can be made to look surprisingly attractive in shows, and for photographs.

The three jump

The waltz jump, more commonly known as the three jump, comprises a half-turn in mid-air, taking off from the forward outside edge of one foot and landing on the back outside edge of the other. It is, like the waltz itself, basically simple, yet possible to improve to such an extent that, with skilful execution, timing, speed and height, its performance can become an outstanding achievement.

Landing on the *toe* of the blade while travelling backwards will cushion the effect and eliminate that harsh, telltale echo produced by a landing on the flat of the blade.

Concentrate on height

First find which way round a jump comes more naturally for you. For most people it is easier to turn anti-clockwise, taking off from the left foot and landing on the right. (Both directions off either foot should be mastered eventually, but this need not concern you yet.)

So, if you start with the left foot, you first glide forward on the outside edge and begin to straighten the skating knee. Then, as the right leg passes it, you spring as high in the air as possible before rotating a half-turn in anti-clockwise direction. You land backwards on the right back outside edge, with the free leg extended behind.

Remember to bend the knees when landing. You must always try to gain as much height as possible from your spring before rotating. It is temptingly easier to jump and rotate without gaining much height, but it does not look nearly so effective.

Spreadeagle and split jumps

Starting from the spreadeagle position, the spreadeagle jump is executed on either the inner or outer edges, and is done by holding the original position until the last moment, when the heels are pulled closer together and a half-turn or full-turn is made in midair while retaining the spread position. It is not easy, requires much patience while learning and depends on your natural ability

Figure 12. The spreadeagle, shown here performed on the inside edges of the skates.

to do an ordinary spread, which varies according to individual physique.

One of the most attractive moves, which seldom fails to please an audience if correctly performed with proper control of the arms and hands, is the split jump. Its fullest effect depends on the extent of your ability to adopt a split position. Take off from a back edge (inner or outer), and land on a forward edge.

Do the spreadeagle or split jumps suit your physique? Slim, long-legged people are usually most suited to these jumps, and many good skaters who find physical difficulty in holding the

Figure 13. The split jump.

spread or split positions do not include the jumps in their repertoire. This is a question of personal trial and decision, but if you
can achieve either jump without undue physical difficulty, they
will certainly add to your performance and be among the most
spectacular movements to watch.

Loop, rocker, counter and bracket jumps

The loop jump, requiring a full revolution in the air, is important
as the basis of several more advanced jumps. The take-off is
from a back outside edge, landing on the same edge of the same
foot. As in all jumps, but particularly so in this one, you have to
guard against rotating too early in order to gain maximum
elevation.

Covering a considerable distance during its execution, the
rocker jump, using the toe point of the free foot, is achieved by
jumping the rocker turn, usually from the back outside edge to
the forward outside edge of the same foot. But it can also be
performed from the forward outside edge, or from forward or

backward inside edges. The inside rocker jump looks particularly attractive, especially if performed across the width of a rink.

The counter jump can also be performed from any of the four edges. In the bracket jump, otherwise known as a choctaw or mohawk jump, you may land on either the same foot or on the opposite foot to that used in the take-off.

Reading descriptions of the more advanced jumps will make you more conscious of what you have to do, but continually jumping incorrectly can harm your style and technique. As always in skating, getting someone more experienced to watch and comment when you practise a new movement will greatly increase the rate of progress. It is worth the expense of having an instructor each time you begin to learn a new jump. Once sure of what you should do, repeated practice is the only way to perform it well.

The lutz jump

From a *fast* back outside spiral, with the skating knee bent as low as possible, the lutz jump take-off is from a back outer edge. Use the toe of the free foot as a lever to describe a full turn in the air in reverse (clockwise) direction, and land on the outside back edge of the opposite foot to that used in the take-off. From the moment of take-off, a peep over the shoulder in the direction of your turn helps smoothness of rotation.

The lutz jump is one of the most difficult to perform really well. Good style, close positioning of the feet in mid-air and graceful arm movements throughout can come only with painstaking practice. That is why a skater is proud to say he can do the lutz. It is a challenge.

The salchow jump

Performed after a forward outside three jump, an almost full turn in the air is accomplished in the advanced salchow jump (originated by the Swede, Ulrich Salchow). Start on the middle of the blade from a back inside edge, and land on the back outside edge of the other skate. Height is much more important than distance. A variation of the salchow, also following a forward outside three jump, but starting from the toe-point, is known as the flip jump.

The axel jump

Perhaps the most famous jump of all, the axel, is named after its Norwegian originator, Axel Paulsen. It requires extra rotation in the air – one and a half turns – starting from a forward outer edge and ending on the back outer edge of the other skate. It is, in fact, a three jump combined with, and continued into, a loop jump.

Doubles and triples

After this, we have such further advanced jumps as the double salchow, double loop, double axel, double lutz, double flip and triple jumps. All show by their names the number of mid-air revolutions involved, and all call for extreme height to give time in which to complete such turns. But multiple jumps are for the championship-class skater, and single jumps need to be mastered first.

Linking together

With the knowledge and ability to do the elementary spirals, jumps and linking steps, and with a groundwork of some of the basic school figures, you can now link some of the moves together and get some feeling of a free-skating programme which, with spins added, will enable you to skate exhibitions and enter competitions. Is fame just round the corner? It may be if you persevere.

Glossary of jumps

The better known and internationally recognized jumps of not less than 360 degrees revolution are listed below, each with its ISU factor for difficulty. Abbreviations used are as follows:

f = forward   b = backward   i = inside   o = outside
n = natural rotation   r = reverse rotation
TA = toe-assisted take-off

Jump	Take-off	Landing	Revolutions	Direction of rotation	ISU factor
Axel Paulsen	fo	bo on opposite foot	$1\frac{1}{2}$	n	3
Double Axel Paulsen	fo	bo on opposite foot	$2\frac{1}{2}$	n	6
One foot Axel Paulsen	fo	bi on same foot	$1\frac{1}{2}$	n	3
Double one foot Axel Paulsen	fo	bi on same foot	$2\frac{1}{2}$	n	6
Inside Axel Paulsen	fi	bo on same foot	$1\frac{1}{2}$	n	3
Double inside Axel Paulsen	fi	bo on same foot	$2\frac{1}{2}$	n	7
Loop	bo	bo on same foot	1	n	2
Double loop	bo	bo on same foot	2	n	5
Triple loop	bo	bo on same foot	3	n	8
Half loop	bo	bi on opposite foot	1	n	2
Double half loop	bo	bi on opposite foot	2	n	4
Toe loop	boTA	bo on same foot	1	n	2
Double toe loop	boTA	bo on same foot	2	n	4
Triple toe loop	boTA	bo on same foot	3	n	8
Lutz	boTA	bo on opposite foot	1	r	3
Double lutz	boTA	bo on opposite foot	2	r	6
Triple lutz	boTA	bo on opposite foot	3	r	8
One foot lutz	boTA	bi on same foot	1	r	3
Double one foot lutz	boTA	bi on same foot	2	r	6
Toeless lutz	bo	bo on opposite foot	1	r	3
Double toeless lutz	bo	bo on opposite foot	2	r	8
Salchow	bi	bo on opposite foot	1	n	2
Double salchow	bi	bo on opposite foot	2	n	4
Triple salchow	bi	bo on opposite foot	3	n	7

Jump	Take-off	Landing	Revolutions	Direction of rotation	ISU factor
One foot salchow	bi	bi on same foot	1	n	2
Double one foot salchow	bi	bi on same foot	2	n	4
Toe salchow	biTA	bo on opposite foot	1	n	2
Double toe salchow	biTA	bo on opposite foot	2	n	5
Walley	bi	bo on same foot	1	r	3
Toe walley	biTA	bo on same foot	1	r	2
Double toe walley	biTA	bo on same foot	2	r	5

11. How to Spin

A reasonable number and variety of spins should be included in any free-skating programme. A good spin is executed on one spot without any 'travel'. The first thing to overcome is dizziness, so look at eye level and not up or down while spinning. Looking at the same fixed point at eye level each time round is a wise habit in ballet and skating rotations.

At first you will tend to rock the body too much, and this exaggerated movement may cause you to feel a little dizzy when starting. This is more often than not a sign that you are not spinning correctly. I emphasize this so that the beginner should not be discouraged. It is just an initial discomfort that the normally healthy, persevering skater will overcome.

It is therefore important to keep the movement of head and body symmetrical, and the shoulders level, while rotating. Sonja Henie, the great skating film star, caught on early to the idea of ending a spin with a definite jerk or toss of the head, which can be not only theatrically effective, but equally successful in 'clearing the cobwebs'.

Once the turn is begun, the skating knee has to be kept rigid, and this applies to both knees in the case of a two-foot spin. No motion of the body should be seen during the rotation of a good spin, other than the drawing in of the arms, after which the *gradual* lowering of the free foot down to beside the spinning ankle can increase momentum.

The things that look best in skating are often the most elementary movements really well done, and this certainly applies to the

Figure 14. The start of a two-foot spin. Note the positions of the arms (left) when preparing to spin, and how they come together (right) when the body swings round.

single flat-foot spin on the flat of the skate, with balance centred over the ball of the foot. A single toe-spin is similarly performed, except that the weight is on the toe-point. Small circles are scratched on the ice during its execution, which is why it is often referred to as a scratch spin.

Remember to hold the head high at the beginning of the spin. To gain momentum, pull in the arms and free leg (in one-foot spins) gradually, not quickly, to the body. When stopping, as the speed slackens take the free foot away from the skating knee and check the rotation by touching the toe-rake on the ice while opening the arms out to the sides and checking the shoulder rotation.

Remember to look at that fixed object each time round to avert giddiness. Be patient. Resist the temptation to hurry, and remember that it takes time to learn to spin properly. Do not practise spinning for too long at a time. Do something else, and return to more spinning later.

The sit spin

Once the simpler spins and jumps have been mastered, and sufficient control and confidence gained, more variety can be

Figure 15. Going into the sit spin. Start with a standing spin and drop into a sitting position, with the free leg extended.

achieved in advanced spins, with arms and free legs in varied positions.

The sit spin, originated by the American, Jackson Haines, starts as a standing spin, the skater immediately afterwards sinking on his skating knee in a sitting posture, with the free leg extended in front. It is important to pull in the stomach and bend the body forward during the lowering movement.

The camel spin

The arabesque spin, which gets its name from a resemblance to the ballet movement, is perhaps better known as the camel spin. It is performed with the torso and free leg parallel to the ice, and the back arched, but there are many variations of arm positions. More advanced still are change-foot spins which, when well executed to a centre, lead to jumping from one spin to the other.

The cross-foot spin

Perhaps the most impressive of all spins is the cross-foot, used so often to end a programme and, if well performed, seldom failing to win loud applause. It seems natural nowadays for a champion's display to finish with a cross-foot spin, and the faster and longer it is the more the crowd like it.

It is widely believed that the toes should be quite together, but a far greater speed can be obtained with the left toes against the right boot, about an inch from the tips of the right toes. Another little trick, which can only be used with perfect control and balance, is to clasp the hands together as soon as they are close enough to do so. This creates a sort of leverage, and the arms can be pulled in much more quickly, which has the effect of giving a sudden burst of speed towards the end of the spin.

After individual spins and jumps have been learned, you can add to your free-skating repertoire by combining a jump and a spin. In this way the flying sit spin and the flying camel have been evolved.

Having learned some spins, you can now include them in a provisional free-skating programme, linking them with spirals and jumps. However limited your ability so far, so long as you can perform the simplest jump, spin and spiral, you can devise some kind of exhibition routine, to which can be added improved technical contents as and when you learn to achieve them.

12. Preparing a Programme

When putting together a free-skating programme, great care should be taken to choose a musical recording of mood, speed and tempo to suit your individual skating style. The length of the recording to be used must be timed to equal the length of the display, which will be dictated by the rules if in a competition. In senior championships, a man has to skate for five minutes and a woman for four; proportionately less for junior events.

In the case of an exhibition, the rink management may stipulate a certain time limit. But, if given a choice, the answer to how long you should skate is how long you know that you can perform without being unduly affected by limitations of strength and stamina.

If your repertoire is definitely restricted, as is usually the case with juniors, it is far better to skate a short, fast, well-varied programme of two minutes rather than lengthen the exhibition without really adding to the technical contents.

With some idea of what you can perform well enough to include in a programme, you must find some suitable music – the right speed, with descriptive beats at suitable intervals so that you can time the landings of your jumps to them.

Music to suit the mood of the programme must be in your mind. There is always a music specialist at a rink, usually the person who operates the recording equipment. Until you are more experienced, consult him about a suitable choice, perhaps after letting him watch you run through your programme.

Arrange for the jumps and spins to be evenly spaced out so that they will not tax your breathing too much.

Question of pattern

Deciding on the *pattern* of a free-skating programme must be one of the most exciting occupations of any truly creative skater. The art of presentation is so often underestimated. In their eagerness to demonstrate their technical ability in jumps and spins, skaters too often disregard the importance of how best to present them – in what sequence and in what part of the rink – to ensure that each speciality is seen to best advantage.

Whether you are performing mainly to satisfy judges or to please the public, a strong start and an impressive finish are important. The obvious first move in planning a programme, therefore, is to arrange for the closing seconds the most imposing and difficult movement you can do well *when slightly tired*, and to try at the beginning the most effective movement you can best skate when fresh.

The rest of the programme should be a blend of highlight jumps and spins at reasonable intervals, linked with attractive steps, spirals and maybe a spread. After the opening movement, give the muscles a moment or two to get thoroughly warmed up before going into more strenuous manoeuvres. Then space the highlights at times in the programme found to suit your personal moments of strength and fatigue. These vary according to each skater's physique and stamina.

Plan and distribute your highlights in suitable and different parts of the rink to show them to full advantage. And plan it so that use is made of all the ice area, thus avoiding any tendency to cramp too much activity into one part of the rink.

Compile a list of technical movements you can perform. Number them, then rewrite the list in what seems to be the best order to perform them. Draw a rectangle to signify the rink, and mark on it the number of each movement in the position considered best to display it.

Quality rather than quantity

The quality should be consistent throughout, but it will not be so if too many of your best movements are crowded too near the beginning of a programme, which can so easily be spoilt by a lukewarm finish.

How many difficult jumps and spins are packed into your programme must depend on your standard and repertoire. Remember that a programme consisting almost entirely of well-performed, neatly planned and simple steps will look better than one containing any difficult movements beyond your capability. In competitions, as many marks are awarded for artistic impression as for technical merit.

When you are more experienced, though, you must be wary not to crowd a programme with too many jumps and spins, however good, at the expense of 'trimmings' and pleasing continuity. An audience can be bored surprisingly quickly through seeing too much of a good thing.

Whatever programme is devised, it should be practised and *memorized* before the day so thoroughly that it can be performed almost subconsciously, without having to keep asking yourself: 'What comes next?'

Include in your programme the things you do best, but do not repeat them as you are only marked for doing them once. Omit those things you know you cannot do properly, and concentrate on doing well what you know well. Quality now, quantity later.

Pleasing the crowd

A vital part of pleasing presentation is 'geographical' planning. Spins and jumps normally look best in the centre of the rink or at either end of it (assuming it is rectangular, as most are). A fast-moving split jump slap in the middle of the rink, performed so that the main body of the audience gets a good profile view, is bound to go well.

The good old cross-foot spin, or a series of two or three axel jumps at either end of the rink or in the centre, are always effective. A sit spin is probably best appreciated if not too far from the spectators, so long as it is not too near the barrier either.

A shrewd variation of the spirals and linking steps should be employed to ensure that an impression is not given of moving too much in the same direction. Every effort should be made to 'fill' the rink surface, using all parts of it with fairly consistent regularity.

An exhibition looks somewhat apologetic when concentrated too much in one area of the rink, leaving parts of it virtually unexplored, to say nothing of causing the sections of onlookers concerned to feel neglected. In your anxiety to fill the skating area, however, it is as well to remember not to go too close to the barrier because, apart from the possible risk of injury through touching it at speed, some of the audience will probably be unsighted.

Variation of tempo is also desirable. While still keeping in time to the music, you can add interest by altering speed, just as a military band commands more attention and admiration by alternating between quick and slow marching.

Practise the happy look

Whether you are in a competition or giving an exhibition, remain aware of the manner of presentation. Concentrating on technique is important, but when doing so you must not *look* too studious or anxious. Practise looking happy, confident and less nervous than you feel, even if it means keeping a fixed 'cheese' smile. In time it will come more naturally, even when feeling butterflies in the stomach. Looking happy and self-assured will pay dividends when the judges award their marks.

13. Further Free-skating Tips

Quite a common oversight leads occasionally to skating 'in the dark'. At some rinks there are 'blind' places which the spotlights cannot reach. It is best to find out where these are beforehand and put up imaginary 'entry forbidden' signs in the appropriate places. I have seen so many stars neglect to take this simple precaution, but it is the seemingly trivial details which, collectively, do really matter.

While on the subject of lighting, I would advocate the use of spotlights for exhibitions as often as is suitable because they focus full attention upon the performer and provide a variation of spectacle. Wise selection of colours can easily enhance the effect, chosen largely according to one's dress and the *mood* to be expressed. Green adds much to a grotesque atmosphere if so desired, red can be dramatic, pink more relaxing, yellow suggests happiness and blue romance.

Many skaters rely too much on their instructors for devising their free-skating programmes, but a really good instructor – in the altruistic sense, that is – will encourage his pupils so far as possible to construct their own routines. Only thus can individual personality be properly expressed. Those who follow skating closely know only too well how stereotyped a performance can get if it reflects only the instructor's thoughts, style and ideas.

If, as soon as one starts skating an exhibition, the tutor's style can be spotted – and, alas, it can far too frequently – it is a sign of lack of individuality and creative thought on the part of the pupil and a sad comment on the ability of his coach. 'Oh, that's so-and-so's pupil – you can see that by his technique' is a criticism far too often justified.

This tendency to produce skaters like 'peas in a pod', expressionless automatons who perform similar routines in more or less the same way, serves only to mark time in, if not actually retard, the progress of skating. After all, free-skating is designed to bring out each skater's own individuality and personality, to give everyone full scope to express *themselves*. If skaters are only copying and repeating movements given them by someone else, it is not really they whom the audience is seeing, but somebody else through them.

As Gladys Hogg once told me, no two skaters really tackle a jump in exactly the same way, and as long as the basic edges are correct they should be encouraged and helped to find the method which suits them best, and should *not* try to copy somebody else. To be one's self and not exactly like anyone else is the first step towards attaining that indefinable asset so invaluable in any kind of public appearance – contemporarily known as a 'gimmick'.

Before competitions, free-skaters are permitted a few minutes' skating in which to 'warm up'. This time is usually most profitably employed by *not* overpractising, but concentrating on keeping the muscles warm and inspecting the entire skating surface, so that, if any parts of it look doubtful, a slight readjustment in approximate positions chosen for the more difficult movements can be devised in one's mind.

Immediately before an exhibition one is bound to experience a certain amount of strain and worry. All true artists do in all branches of entertainment and one never altogether overcomes the feeling of butterflies in the stomach before the start. Once begun, however, all that miraculously disappears. It is the same for a boxer before he enters the ring and for a footballer before he emerges from the tunnel, but, once the action has begun, nerves – or is it apprehension? – disappear like magic.

Keep warm and well wrapped up until the last possible moment before going on the ice. A smallish meal two hours before the event is wise. Never skate on an empty stomach. A coffee is good just before skating, though many prefer an orange just to moisten the throat.

Choose music to suit your individual free-skating style, with dramatic effects to which your jumping and spinning highlights may be spectacularly timed. Changing tempos to coincide with varying pace and moods must also be considered.

Select a 'hummable' melody likely to have a psychologically pleasing effect on the audience and judges. This helps everyone to pay full attention to the skating. Music difficult to understand at the outset can tend to cause concentration to stray from the actual skating.

Be conscious of your music at all times. 'Feel' its beat with every skating stroke you take.

An attractive, lively opening, giving an early idea of range in jumps, spins and linking steps, can often put audience and judges in an alert, interested mood of pleasant anticipation.

Element of surprise

One should aim for original touches whenever possible. Foot-work preceding and linking jumps, spins and other special contents should be varied to introduce as much an element of surprise as one is capable of introducing.

Strive for the unexpected sometimes. Getting away from the stereotyped 'run of the mill' exhibition will cause onlookers to sit up and take more notice.

Try to avoid 'telegraphing' the next move to prevent those watching from realizing too early what is coming. Fool the on-looker's predictions and originality will progress.

Always be ready to cope with emergencies by carrying duplicates. A costume damaged *en route*, a broken zip, a torn lace, a mislaid or damaged record or tape may render all the painstaking practice fruitless if you do not have the foresight and enterprise to have a second dress in reserve, another disc or tape and a spare pair of laces.

Having a tape as well as a record is a prudent precaution to solve any local sound system difficulty.

Carry a small screwdriver and skate screws. A *new* pair of laces for a competition or exhibition can prove to be a profitable

5. Masters of the death spiral. Top: Oleg Protopopov and Ludmila Belousova (USSR). Centre: Alexei Ulanov and Irina Rodnina (USSR). Below: Ken Shelley and Jo Jo Starbuck (USA).

6. *Far left:* Ondrej Nepela, thrice Czechoslovakia's world champion, 1971–3

7. *Left:* Toller Cranston, Canada's world bronze medallist, 1974.

8. *Below, left:* Precision and glamour in the sumptuously attired skating corps de ballet are striking features of the spectacular 'Holiday on Ice' shows constantly touring the world. The straw boaters were worn in a skating tribute to Maurice Chevalier.

9. *Below:* Christine Errath, East Germany's world champion, 1974.

10. A desperate ice hockey save from Finnish forwards by Leif Holmqvist, Swedish goalminder for London Lions, founder members of the new European League. Note the goalie's protective face mask.

11. Monkey business on ice. Jackie the chimp skating for peanuts in an ice show.

investment. Keep your essential equipment with you when travelling. Do not risk losing anything on the journey.

It is wise to take an extra pair of tights and, of course, needles, thread and pins in readiness for that unexpectedly but always inopportune loose hem or button.

Everyone has a favourite pair of skates and many would be completely at a loss if these were damaged, lost or stolen. Such a dilemma could be overcome by having identical pairs and wearing and breaking in each set alternately during the same period of time.

The knowledge that you are prepared for any emergency has a tonic effect on one's peace of mind.

Do not rely implicitly on an alarm clock for an important morning when you are due to skate early. Have a friend double-check to make sure you wake at the right time.

You cannot relax properly before an event if you have to worry about the time factor, so always allow more time than normally necessary in order to avoid being flustered by a traffic hold-up or unforeseen last-minute occurrence.

Before visiting a strange rink for a competition, check on that rink's ice surface area to be sure in advance that either your routine is suitable for those dimensions or, if necessary, can be adapted accordingly.

When you make a mistake in a competition or proficiency test, forget it at once and concentrate entirely on what you are immediately required to do. Never brood or reflect on an error until after the event is over.

Keep warm just before you are due to go on the ice. Limber up with elementary exercises. This helps one to relax and, at the same time, keeps the muscles supple. A muscle is more likely to be pulled when it is cold or taut.

Never wear a dress for the first time in a competition. It is too late then to discover a fault in fitting which may only become apparent during a skating movement.

Never publicly display annoyance at what you consider to be a bad decision. A sporting loser and a modest winner in the long run always gain the greatest public respect and popularity.

Critics aid progress

Get experienced friends to watch your style and posture. You cannot see yourself as others do. Constructive criticism can greatly accelerate progress.

To improve erect carriage and graceful arm and hand movements, try practising sometimes with objects balanced on the head and also on the backs of the hands.

The art of pair skating has been much neglected. The opportunities of winning distinction in this branch of the sport are correspondingly greater. Initial selection of a partner is all-important. Pay special attention to the questions of blending dispositions, temperaments, common interests, similarity in style and suitability in height. The man should be, ideally, about two inches taller.

The man should be at all times 'captain' of a pair. He must do the leading and learn to show off his partner to the best effect. The careers of many a promising pair have been marred by clashing temperaments and, consequently, quarrelsome nagging.

Make sure you get on well together off the ice as well as on it before committing yourself to a regular partner.

Once you are satisfied with the composition of a programme, keep going through it until you can memorize every detail. Running through it two or three times in succession not only helps this, but also conditions the stamina and staying power.

Remove your skate-guards at the last moment before stepping on to the ice and leave them ready at the rinkside to put on immediately after stepping off the ice. The result: no rust, no nicks from wood or concrete flooring – and appreciably longer life for your skates.

Is weight your problem? The types of carbohydrate food to cut down on are well known, but remember also to eat less bulk, whatever the type of food. The more one eats, the more the stomach muscles extend and, in consequence, the more one feels the need for food. Conversely, the less one eats, the more the stomach muscles contract and the appetite lessens.

14. Choosing the Music

A constant envelopment in the sport has advanced this mere male's ability to describe the most intricate details of feminine attire – for skating, that is. Even more, it has taught me very much about relevant musical appreciation, particularly when producing and compèring a weekly radio programme. This series of broadcasts comprised interviews with famous skaters, interspersed with music to which they skated, and the scope for musical entertainment available from such programmes was remarkably wide.

I was not ashamed of the unoriginal signature tune. Even if you are a little tired of hearing Waldteufel's the 'Skater's Waltz', do please listen to the instrumentally superb recording of it by the Boston Promenade Orchestra, and to the more recent version by the Band of the Royal corps of signals. Both make fine accompaniments for skaters of all grades.

Certainly we had variety, too, varying from 'The Sabre Dance', Saint-Saëns's 'The Swan' and Gounod's 'Ballet Music from *Faust*' to the contrasting rhythmic tempo of Glenn Miller's 'In the Mood'.

Denis Bird, a longstanding friend and respected journalistic confrère, whose musical knowledge through following skating has escalated well beyond mine, once aptly wrote: 'There is one factor which lifts skating right out of the realm of sport and entitles it to a rightful place among the fine arts; the requirement that all free and pair skating shall be executed to music, like a ballet solo or *pas de deux*.'

Music, of course, is an integral part of every free-skating

programme. The right choice of appropriate accompaniment is vital and I will go so far as to suggest that, without a natural love and ear for music, real stardom on skates is as inaccessible as it is to those who give no attention to ballet movements. Each step, every jump and spin, must be placed appropriately to time with the music, and this is something that honestly cannot be taught. One is born with or without appreciable musical sense and I am truly sorry for those who cannot fully endorse the sentiment that 'life is nothing without music'.

The choice of musical accompaniment entails selecting a piece not only with the right-timed beats and changes of tempo to suit one's skating repertoire. Its length must synchronize precisely with the duration of the performance so that skater and record (or selected part of it) finish simultaneously. It must inspire the skater, help his sense of interpretation and please his audience.

Personally, I would advocate always 'playing safe' in the latter respect by using something that is either easily recognized or certain to be well liked, rather than anything obscure or little known, whether it be 'pop' or classical. Above all, the need to associate the timing of every skating movement with the right beat of music cannot be overstressed.

The music must express the mood required, whether it be gaiety, humour, sadness, vivacity, strength, or dignity, and so ease the task of self-expression by miming gestures of the arms, hands, fingers, head, face, shoulders, hips, even knees – all have a part to play.

Let it never be said that only the feet matter in free-skating. The really technically minded may, consciously or not, watch the feet of the performer throughout an exhibition, but I think it sometimes can be rather a nice compliment for an artist to be told: 'Your display was so fascinating that I almost forgot you were on skates at all.' By which I mean that it is also very important what goes on *above* those skates.

A permanent 'cheesy' smile or inane grin throughout is at least more desirable than any expression of concern about one's skating, but emotion can be expressed so well in the face and a variety of emotions to interpret the music or story as the exhibition progresses is the all-too-rare ideal.

Arm and body movements from the waist upwards are of immense importance and for that reason a knowledge of ballet is an enormous asset to any skater. I know of no really successful skater who has not studied ballet at least a little. Gloria Nord, who spent eight years under an American ballet tutor specializing in arm and hand movements, showed what can be achieved in this respect in her memorable portrayal of Marjanah in *Chu Chin Chow* on ice.

Here was an extreme example of how ballet training dominated skating ability. In Gloria's case it had to, for she never took a skating test or entered a competition in her life. Conversely, some champion skaters have proved to be ice show failures, largely due to their neglect of theatrical showmanship or movements from the waist upwards.

It is interesting to note, however, that Jacqueline du Bief, whose creative sense of interpretation on skates was, to my mind, in a class of its own, did *not* strongly advocate *practical* ballet tuition for skaters so much as frequently *watching* ballets performed.

Most championship competitors naturally prefer to skate to their own chosen recording rather than to a 'live' orchestra and so eliminate any risk of misunderstanding. An element of human error is possible in the best orchestra, but one always knows what will come on a familiar record, provided there is no technical hitch. The fullest instructions with regard to speed, where to start and so on obviously should be made absolutely clear to whoever is responsible for operating the rink record-player.

The uninitiated spectator may now understand and sympathize more with the competitor whose record may be somewhat scratchy during a championship. Even television commentators have had to apologize occasionally for 'music not up to the usual standard'. This is because it is not unusual for a skater to have welded his free-skating programme to an old and treasured, out-of-stock recording which he has belatedly discovered cannot easily be duplicated nor improved upon by having it copied.

For exhibitions, when marks are not sought and errors are to a degree less important, 'live' orchestral accompaniment where convenient is sometimes desired – unless, that is, the orchestra leader is not sufficiently conversant with skating tempi or temperaments, in which case heaven help him, the skaters and the rink management.

The scope of suitable music for skating is surprisingly wide. It is by no manner of means confined to dreamy waltzes, as some non-skaters still seem to suppose, and, as was implied at the beginning of this chapter, one's knowledge of music can expand enormously as a result of following what is used for skating.

For many enthusiasts, Cecilia Colledge drew much closer attention to the beautiful 'Dream of Olwen'. But for Bridget Shirley-Adams's charming interpretation, I should probably never have learned to like 'Clair de Lune' so much. Graham Sharp and Daphne Walker in the same way commanded increased respect for George Gershwin's 'Rhapsody in Blue'.

Those not already aware of it may be startled to know that Barbara Ann Scott skated publicly to 'Ave Maria', and Tenley Albright to 'Ol' Man River'. For a light-hearted encore, Dick Button had many a packed audience clapping loudly to time while he skated to 'American Patrol'. Typical of suitable music in more serious vein are the 'Polovtsian Dances' from *Prince Igor,* Strauss's lovely 'Der Rosenkavalier' waltz, and Bizet's *Carmen* to which Don Jackson skated passionately to such great effect.

If pop stars can plug their latest LP, surely I can too. My special selection of melodies with a skating theme has been recorded by the Band of the Royal Corps of Signals under the direction of Major Keith Boulding. You will find in this a military-style version of the 'Skater's Waltz' and many pieces which famous skaters have used for their championship programmes. The disc is being released by Decca to synchronise with the publication of this book – and with the same title, *Let's Go Skating.*

Each skater should seek his own inspiration and discover the right kind of accompaniment to fit in with his style of performance and timing. It soon gets to the stage when, consciously or subconsciously, one finds nearly every radio or television programme dominated by personal thoughts concerning this or that piece of music's possible suitability for a skating routine.

Remarks on costumes in a previous chapter were intended for competitive free-skating and the more authentic, classical style of exhibition. But otherwise, for displays aimed essentially to please the public, originality and innovations are ever welcome. If one can tell a story in mime and wear appropriate attire, or merely if one dresses according to the music – a national costume to, say, Swiss or Dutch melodies, a sailor's uniform for nautical music, etc. – the scope is infinite.

Props, too, can be used to immense advantage. As an Easter chick, one can emerge from an enormous egg; as a golly from a jack-in-the-box; a huntsman can wield his post-horn; and so on. Something novel by which the skater will be remembered additional to his actual skating is surely the right aim for the ambitious who want to get known and win more invitations to perform.

Should one fall, never let it disturb – outwardly or inwardly. Time and again a smile and a quick recovery bring more spontaneous, admiring applause from the audience than might have been the case if a tumble had not occurred. It reminds and emphasizes the hazards of skating, and I hope this thought will inspire many who fall not to let it rattle them and, after recovery, to forget all about it until reminded the following morning by the only real black mark likely to result.

In case so much detail about free-skating may suggest that it is all a very serious business indeed, let it be stressed that, far from it, free-skating above all else should be thoroughly enjoyed – and that enjoyment should be reflected by relaxed movements and happy facial expressions. But that does not preclude the most painstaking preparation, for still fuller pleasure will accompany the outlook that 'what is worth doing is worth doing well'.

15. Togetherness

The regulations for ice pair skating require the two partners to perform movements that give a homogeneous impression. Although both partners need not always perform similar movements and may separate from time to time, they must convey a sense of unison and harmonious composition.

Lifts, spins, jumps, spirals, spreads and all other free-skating actions are permissible. Skaters have limited freedom of choice to incorporate any known or new movement, the guiding factor being this homogeneous impression, or 'togetherness' as it might be more simply termed.

Competitions are divided into two sections, the short programme and free-skating, each to music. For the former, pairs are required to skate six compulsory moves with connecting steps, their skill in performing them being worth a quarter of the contest's total marks.

The free-skating is left to the skaters' choice except for specified limitations, which restrict some of the more hazardous movements sometimes seen in professional ice shows. For example, revolutions are forbidden in which one partner, supported by the other, stays off the ice for a period exceeding that required for the completion of a continuous combined skating movement.

If the jumping partner is assisted in a jump by the other partner, as in a lift, the jump as a whole must consist of one continuous ascending and descending rotational movement. For all pair skating lifts the partners may give each other assistance only through hand-to-hand, hand-to-arm and hand-to-body grips. Assistance by holding the legs is forbidden.

Lifts in which the carrying partner executes more than three complete revolutions including changes of hold are also forbidden. The simple carrying of a partner including carrying with extended arms is not allowed. Spinning moves in which the man swings the lady around in the air while holding her by the hand or foot are not permitted. Also forbidden are: the turning of one of the partners in the horizontal position; the jumps of one of the partners towards the other; and rotational movements with the grip of one of the partners on the leg, arm or neck of the other. Nevertheless, the so-called 'death spiral', in which the lady circles round the man with at least one foot on the ice, is permitted.

'Shadow skating' is the term generally applied to those parts of the pairs programme where both skaters perform with unity of movement but while separated – that is, not touching.

Pair skating essentially requires teamwork in every sense. Ideally, the man should be slightly taller and the couple should match in ability and appearance to pleasing effect. One has to concentrate not only on proficiency of movement but on proficiency of synchronization with one's partner, both in timing and so that inclination of arms, hands, legs and feet correspond.

Each must learn to understand the partner's movements and ability so that they can anticipate and match each other's every step with precision. For that reason, it is imperative that the performance be kept within the limitations of the technically weaker partner.

'Filling' the rink area during a free-skating performance is just as important for a pair as it is in planning soloist programmes. Among the best known specialized pair skating highlights, as distinct from synchronized solo shadow movements, are the death spiral, the lasso lift, the overhead axel lift, the split lutz lift and the catch waist camel spin.

The *death spiral* is the popular name given to a movement whereby the man swings his partner round at very great speed while retaining virtually the same pose, the girl apparently risking 'death' by her repetitive proximity to the ice while revolving round her partner and, in the process, sometimes allowing her hair to touch the ice. The styles can be varied with one- or two-

F

handed holds in various grips. Controlled wrist and arm strength and centrifugal force are prime factors.

In the single *lasso lift,* from a side-by-side, hand-to-hand position, the lady is lifted overhead in an outside forward take-off. turning one and a half rotations with the man's arms stretched (lasso pose) and the lady's legs in split position. The man remains forward to complete a backward landing on the right outside edge.

In the spectacular *axel lift,* the girl is turned one and a half times completely over her partner's head. After holding hands on one side, she is supported in the lift by the man's hand under her armpit. The lift begins from the girl's outside forward edge and is completed on the outside back edge of her opposite skate. The man rotates beneath the girl throughout the movement.

To achieve the *split lutz lift,* both partners start from a side-by-side position, travelling backwards. The girl is lifted from an outside back edge. During the lift she assumes a split lutz position. At the conclusion of the lift she is travelling on a back outside edge and the man on a forward outside edge.

Always agreeable to watch, the *catch waist camel* (arabesque) *spin* is performed with the free legs pointing in opposite directions, the bodies close together and arms around each other's waist. The spin by each partner is executed on the flat of the blade while the torso and free leg are parallel to the ice, with the back arched.

Before 1964, senior pair skating championships comprised solely a five-minute programme for each partnership. The additional 'short programme' of connecting compulsory movements must not exceed two and a half minutes' duration. It requires each partnership to demonstrate ability in specified elements of lifts, jumps, spins, spirals and connecting steps. The elements are drawn each season from one of four groups.

Not only is this test of quality very interesting to technicians. The onlooking layman is more easily able to identify and appreciate each type of movement. The only other apparent justifiable reason for adding this compulsory section would seem to be that the judges are otherwise unable to interpret and assess with sufficient accuracy all that they see in the main free-skating presentation.

The marks for both sections, as for solo free-skating, are awarded in two sets, each up to six from each judge, the first set for technical merit and the second for artistic presentation.

Pair skating, compared to ice dancing, requires an added degree of strength and athleticism which makes this branch of the sport a particularly thrilling spectacle for the onlooker.

16. Where the Marks Go

Figure skating championships, competitions or proficiency tests are divided into two distinct sections. The first, compulsory figures, requires solo competitors to trace with their skates on the ice specific lobed figures, drawn from an internationally recognized schedule. The second, two-phase section, free-skating, provides in the main phase up to five minutes for men and four minutes for women to skate a programme of their own creation.

Not surprisingly, the majority of spectators watch only the latter stages of a contest. The spectacular appeal of jumps and spins can magnetize capacity stadium crowds and millions of televiewers, but the figures which precede all this usually take place at a comparatively deserted rink, in a hushed atmosphere of almost cathedral-like dignity.

Pair skaters have to perform, instead of figures, six prescribed free-skating movements separately from their main free-skating programme. The compulsory figures vary greatly in degree of difficulty, and are drawn to suit the standard of the event. Each figure is skated three times, each tracing an indentation on the ice. The judges, varying from three to nine, are concerned not only with the merits of the tracings, but also with the skater's control, position and balance. The positions of hands, fingers and non-skating foot are taken into consideration, also a smooth, steady speed and a change from one foot to the other by a single stroke from the skate edge and not from the toe.

When the skater completes a figure, the judges converge on the tracing. They stoop and sometimes even get down on their hands and knees to examine the pattern left by the sharp edges of the skate. The print left on the ice is of prime concern, followed closely by carriage and flow of movement. A bulge in a circle, a 'flatting' of the skate or an improper change from one blade edge to the other will cost tenths of points. Points up to a maximum of six are awarded by each judge for each figure, and these marks are subsequently multiplied by a factor, according to the recognized standard of the figure.

Technique in your compulsory figures can best be checked by your instructor. But you can profitably improve your marks potential by concentrating on style. Think of the parts of the body which do not do the actual skating – the free leg, the arms, hands and fingers, the shoulders, hips and the head. There is a correct position for all of them.

Make sure to learn exactly where each part of the body ought ideally to be for each figure during each part of that figure. Pay special attention to the arms and hands. If these are in the wrong position, the whole effect of the figure can look quite ugly and your balance will be more difficult to control.

Two sorts of freestyle marks

Marks for free-skating are awarded in two sets, separately assessing technical merit and artistic impression. Scoring is again graded up to a maximum six, and the totals multiplied by a factor to ensure they correspond to the marks awarded for figures. The judges have to assess the variation of contents, degree of difficulty and manner of performance.

For example, was speed gathered without visible effort? Did the skater mix in original footwork on toes and edges? Were there smooth transitions and changes in tempo, with sudden surprise movements? Was the skater always in proper position, with toes pointed and back straight? Did the skater make intelligent use of the entire ice area? And did his performance give the feeling of being planned and skated to the music, rather than of being a set show where the music was only incidental?

Take each of the above questions in turn. Can you honestly

answer 'yes' to every one of them? Each question may draw your attention to a shortcoming in your free-skating routine. By concentrating particularly on each one of them, the general appearance of your whole programme must improve.

The free-skating is worth 60 per cent of the total marks and the figure 40 per cent. The free-skating is divided into two phases, a short programme of six prescribed movements, for 20 per cent of the total marks and the final main programme (senior men and pairs, five minutes; women, four) for the other 40 per cent. The shorter programme, regarded by some as repetitively superfluous, has only been in operation since September 1972.

For general guidance to judges, the ISU regulations broadly categorize the marks between 0 and 6 as follows: 0 = not skated, 1 = bad, 2 = unsatisfactory, 3 = mediocre, 4 = good, 5 = very good, 6 = faultless.

A disturbing recent trend in international championships has been an abuse of the maximum six. This once revered score used to imply perfection and, in consequence, was so rarely awarded that its recipients felt justly proud. A regrettable devaluation of the top mark reached the height of absurdity at the 1972 Sapporo Olympics, when Janet Lynn of the United States fell heavily from a jump-sit spin, yet scored a six for artistic merit.

Nearly as blatant in the 1973 European championships at Cologne were three errors by the Russian pair, Alexandr Zaitsev and Irina Rodnina, yet they received the unprecedented award of twelve sixes. The farcical pattern followed in the world championships the same year at Bratislava, when once more Miss Lynn got a six after two-footing a double axel.

The universally admired Janet at the time was unquestionably the world's best woman free-skater and, I believe, charmingly honest enough to have been embarrassed, as indeed were all fair-minded Americans. One hopes a new directive to judges may yet restore the dignity and respect which a six once had.

17. Dancing on Ice

A man and a woman are skating in partnership. Are they pair skating or ice dancing? That is a natural question for the casual onlooker.

Free dancing, as distinct from skating one specific dance, is still strictly limited to acceptable dance movements. The rule-book states that, for competition or test purposes, the free dance shall consist of non-repetitive combinations of new or known dance movements composed into a programme which displays the personal ideas of the dancers in concept and in arrangement.

The free dance must be constructed so that the element of competitive dancing is predominant and so that the free dance shall not have the character of a pair free-skating programme. In the free dance, the competitors' general knowledge and ability in dancing, as well as the originality and concept of their ideas, are evaluated.

Feats of strength and skating skill which do not form part of the dance sequence, but which are inserted to show physical prowess, are counted against the competitors using them.

Certain free-skating movements such as turns, arabesques, pivots, etc., are permitted with the following limitations:

(*a*) Separations of partners for steps, arabesques, pivots, etc., are permitted for not longer than five seconds. A separation during the final sequence of the dance is permitted for not longer than eight seconds.

(*b*) Arabesques and pivots may not exceed the duration of the movements of the compulsory dances.

(*c*) Pirouettes may not exceed three revolutions.

(*d*) Skating on toe picks may not be done excessively.

(*e*) Short jerky movements are acceptable only when they emphasize the character of the music.

(*f*) Stops, in which couples remain stationary on the ice surface while performing body or twist movements or poses, may not exceed two measures of music.

(*g*) Small dance lifts, in which the man may not raise his hands higher than his waistline, are permitted provided they fit the character of the music or emphasize certain passages of the music. These lifts may not have more than one and a half revolutions.

(*h*) Small low dance jumps, for the purpose of changing the foot or direction of one of the partners, are permitted provided that they do not exceed one-half of a revolution and that they are executed in dance position or at not more than two arm-lengths. Both partners may not jump at the same time.

(*i*) A free dance programme which contains too many lifts or jumps, etc., represents more pair skating than free dancing and consequently shall be penalized by the judges.

The above extracts from the regulations are included here to stress the difference between the two kinds of skating in partnership.

It is curious that only since the Second World War has ice dancing become numerically popular. For the masses, participation at public rink sessions has such a social appeal today that probably at least one in every five who set out to learn to skate does so primarily with ambitions to take part in rink ice dancing. Preliminary skating instruction is regarded by many impatient beginners merely as a means to this end.

The need for lessons is similar to the requirements in ballroom dancing. Just as one who has never danced before can hardly expect to cope at the local ballroom, so a skater requires elementary tuition before participating in rink dances. But, as in ordinary dancing, provided the learner possesses the basic essentials of sense of rhythm and ear for the beat, few lessons are required to enable enjoyable participation as distinct from polished performance. In fact, an instructress has told me about a teenage pupil who, starting as a complete novice, grasped the basic steps of no fewer than three dances in six twenty-minute lessons.

The most popular skating dance of all has been the European waltz, the earliest standardized dance and the easiest to learn fundamentally; the most graceful and rhythmical, yet it is no mean achievement to perform the waltz really well. The initial hazard seems to be the tendency to hurry, through anticipating the beat. Smooth, clean turns should be essayed, with threes (half-turns from one edge to the opposite edge on the same foot) turned between the partners' feet.

If possible, as in ballroom dancing, it is advisable to learn with reasonably experienced partners, and there are usually plenty of these ready to encourage the learners in public rink sessions. The instructions for executing all the steps of every ice dance are fully set out and illustrated by diagrams in a standard ISU approved booklet, obtainable from national skating associations. It is not my purpose to reiterate the text, but the following brief description of the accepted waltz hold may helpfully provide many readers with a clearer visual picture.

The man's right hand should hold his partner firmly between the shoulder blades. The lady's left hand should rest equally firmly a little below her partner's right shoulder, her left elbow resting on his right elbow. The man's left arm and the lady's right arm should be extended and held sufficiently firmly to enable synchronized movement.

A couple should skate as closely together as possible in order to retain proper control. It is a common error, when learning, to hold one's partner at too much distance. The back should be arched and the chest thrown out. The body should be carried erect and over the employed skate, checking any inclination to bend forward at the waist.

We are told that Samuel Pepys danced on the ice with Nell Gwynn in London during the Great Frost of 1683, but ice dancing in any form resembling that which is recognized today did not become apparent for another two hundred years, when early inspiration came from the waltz-struck, Strauss-minded Vienna Skating Club in the 1880s.

There is evidence of the waltz being skated on ice at Halifax,

Nova Scotia, as early as 1885 and of an exhibition waltz demon-
strated at the Palais de Glace, Paris, in 1894, which may well have
incited its early popularity in London.

The first organized set-pattern dance specially for skaters was
the ten-step, now more generally called the fourteen-step because
the initial chassé is repeated. It was originated in 1889 by a
Viennese, Franz Schöller, and was sometimes called the Schöller
march. Common errors to counter in this dance occur in the
execution of mohawks (half-turns from an edge of one foot to
the same edge of the other foot), the man's tendency to double
track (skate on both feet simultaneously) in backward movements
and the lady's inclination to lean forward on backward chassés.

In addition to the waltz and fourteen-step, thirteen other
standard ice dances are recognized internationally. The lively
kilian, invented by Karl Schreiter, emerged from Vienna in 1909.
The tango, jointly created by Trudi Harris and Paul Kreckow in
1931, came as a welcome variation and is most attractive when
well performed.

A foxtrot was invented in 1933 by Erik Van der Weyden and his
wife, Eva Keats. With partners close together, the foxtrot is seen
at its best when executed with strong, well-curved edges. It ex-
presses the syncopation of modern foxtrot music, skated not in
the facing waltz position, but side by side, comparable to the
'conversation' position in the ballroom. Thus, with the man's
right hip touching the lady's right, the man's right hand goes on
his partner's right shoulder blade and the lady's left hand is
placed on his shoulder. The man's left hand holds his partner's
right hand, extended in front.

The popular blues to slow music was originated the following
year by Robert Dench and Lesley Turner. Skated with bold
edges, important here is mastery of the choctaw (a half-turn
from an edge on one foot to the opposite edge on the other foot).

Other major dances were conceived in 1934 by the Van der
Weydens. These were the rocker foxtrot, which allows an attractive flowing movement, and the high-spirited Viennese waltz,
danced at a good pace with strongly curved edges.

The same couple in 1938 introduced the Westminster waltz,
part of which is skated in kilian position, using the thumb pivot

grip for the hands to facilitate the changes of sides by the partners. The lady's hands are held above the man's, with the thumbs extended downwards into the man's fists.

Three more dances were added in 1938 by Reg Wilkie and Daphne Wallis, the British champions from 1937 to 1946. They designed the Argentine tango – a difficult set-pattern dance performed at accelerated speed; the relatively simple quickstep; and the speedy, circular paso doble, which, as Wilkie himself observed, is 'quite an easy dance to do badly'.

Yet another dance invented in London in 1938 was the somewhat unorthodox but impressive rumba, devised by Walter Gregory. Another important dance is the American waltz, of uncertain origin. Later dances to gain prominence were the Starlight waltz and the Silver samba, both invented in 1963 by Courtney Jones and Peri Horne. The Starlight waltz is particularly pleasing to the eye, lovely to skate to and, most important of all, relatively easy to perform.

Graduated proficiency tests, for which certificates and medals are awarded in figure skating, are organized nationally for ice dancing, too, with dances suitably divided into levels of difficulty. All dances progress in a counter-clockwise direction round the rink.

Championship events are divided into two halves, one half featuring compulsory dances and the other free dancing. Each of these sections is worth half of the total marks and, as in figure skating, each performance is assessed by a panel of judges.

The compulsory section is quite straightforward, each couple skating three specific dances drawn from an international schedule, and an original set-pattern dance of their own choice, but to a specified rhythm, e.g. waltz or tango.

For senior international and national championships, the initial three dances are any one of three groups of three, drawn just prior to the event. These groups are:

Group 1 Viennese waltz, kilian and quickstep.
Group 2 Westminster waltz, paso doble and blues.
Group 3 Starlight waltz, rumba and Argentine tango.

Unlike the compulsory section, which requires a set sequence of steps, the free-dancing section should ideally consist of a non-repetitive performance of novel movements and variations of known dances. These should be combined in a programme with originality of design and arrangement.

The judges give one set of marks for each of the three compulsory dances and two sets for the set-pattern dance, which, apart from the rhythm, is not 'compulsory' in the same sense as the others. The three first dances are thus together worth 30 per cent of the total and the set-pattern dance 20 per cent.

The free-dancing (four minutes for each couple in major championships) is also accorded two sets of marks which are afterwards multiplied by 2·5 to make 50 per cent of the total.

The first of the two sets of marks for the set-pattern dance are awarded for *composition,* when the judges consider originality, difficulty, variety; correct timing to the music; the movements of the couple in rhythm with the music and the relationship of this movement to the character of the music; and the correct selection of music in relation to the rhythm decreed.

The second mark is for *presentation,* when points assessed are the placement of the steps; cleanness, sureness and utilization of space; and the style of the couple as shown by their carriage, flow and unison.

For the free-dancing, the first set of marks are for *technical merit,* when judges evaluate difficulty, variety, clearness and sureness. The second set is for *artistic impression,* when they look for harmonious composition, conformity to the music, use of space, easy movement and sureness in timing, carriage, originality and expression of the character of the music.

Belated Olympic Status

Although ice dancing is not yet an Olympic sport, its belated inclusion in the Olympic schedule has been agreed, with effect from the 1976 Innsbruck Games. Since 1952, the event has been one of the recognized four which comprise the annual world ice figure and dance skating championships organized by the ISU.

Repeated recommendations by the ISU to the International

Olympic Committee previously had been rejected, partly because of the trend to reduce the overall number of events and participants and partly because the word dancing had not been favourably regarded, but happily there has been a change of heart.

18. Judge and Be Judged

At any figure skating championship, one is naturally often asked by perplexed newcomers to unveil the mysteries of how the results are determined. At the outset, it has to be emphasized that neither the skater with the highest number of points, nor the one with the lowest number of placements (ordinals) is necessarily the winner. That in itself is enough to make any sports editor squirm.

The poor questioner then tries to grasp the fact that the final order is resolved only by majority placings, which broadly means that, whatever the marks awarded, the winner has to be placed first by more judges than any other, and so on down the list.

This, for the uninitiated, is complicated enough to grasp. But when it comes to factorizing down some marks and not others, to adjust to the correct overall percentages for figures and free-skating, is it any wonder that few but the fervent connoisseurs even bother to fathom what inevitably entails considerable mathematical calculations?

The public at large, as distinct from the relatively small 'in-crowd', enjoy what is seen but is incapable of working out the result. If special computers are not used, the full classified scores and positions are sometimes unobtainable hours after an event has ended.

Even the Press is lamentably disregarded by some of the less experienced organizers, lacking a proper sense of urgency. The importance of good public relations are too often overlooked or simply not understood. Skating competitions are notorious for late night finishes. If the convenience of public transport and the news media were considered more carefully, an earlier conclusion so often could be reached through generally better planned timing.

An important international competition held recently, ended just after midnight, not an uncommon occurrence. By 2.30 a.m., a cluster of tired journalists were still waiting for the full results in an otherwise well-organized Press room. Had I not finally chanced to catch the referee getting into his car and had he not been a personal friend, those results would not have appeared in any newspaper the following day – in which case those very organizers, whose fault it would have been, doubtless would have been the first people to suffer.

Does figure skating really have to be besmirched with a mad scramble to ascertain a competitor's standing at any time? It is a major reason why newspapers and television companies give the sport far less space and time than they might do otherwise.

Figure and dance skating judges are voluntary unpaid experts who give their services and time to a sport which is entirely dependent on them. What do the judges get in return?

On the credit side, the satisfaction of letting their experience benefit others and the social enjoyment of mingling with fellow enthusiasts. On the debit side, they lay themselves constantly open to suspicions, if not accusations, of bias or collusion to influence a result.

International judges whose marks vary considerably from the majority are quite normally the subject of routine discussions by a special committee appointed by the ISU for this purpose. Suspensions which sometimes follow such investigations emphasize how anxious the ISU is to keep discrepancies to a minimum and thus preserve the sport's good name.

Incompetence or ignorance of technicalities are quite often found to be the cause of erratic marking rather than ulterior motives. There may be a rotten apple in any barrel and ISU suspension is the penalty when proved, but unfounded suspicions of dishonesty can accrue largely from weaknesses in the present scoring system.

Doubting tongues have long wagged admonishingly at the

frequently suspected, highly complicated methods of deciding the outcome in figure and dance skating championships. The embarrassing position in which judges find themselves with regard to the marks they award compatriots is, and always has been, a major headache. A judge should be given freedom to mark exactly as he or she thinks fit within a system which allows more margin for individual discrepancies than at present.

The present system of majority placings is far too complicated for the inexpert spectator, whose support skating needs to attract and retain. There is thus a growing feeling that the present system should be abolished if a suitable, simpler alternative can be found. One prominent ISU official has stated: 'The rule book should be half as thick but twice as clear.'

My suggested solution is a far simpler system, fairer and more 'fool-proof' than the present one, leaving less scope for judges' embarrassment and more scope for their freedom to mark as they think fit. And, furthermore, a system completely releasing all judges from the always difficult obligation of marking skaters from their own nation.

How can all this be achieved? This three-point answer is disarmingly elementary:

1. Take ten judges from the ten highest placed nations in the corresponding event of the previous season.

2. Nominate the tenth on a rotational basis as a substitute judge, who each time (when applicable) replaces the judge whose own national skater is to be marked.

3. From each set of nine judges' marks throughout the competition, delete the two highest and the two lowest (or two of the highest and lowest in case of equality). This idea is used very successfully in high diving and ski jumping. Thus, only the five middle sets of marks would count each time and their aggregates determine the final order. Place majorities would cease to be applicable.

Note that the first point above would terminate the present tiresome waste of sending some judges 'on spec' just in case they are drawn to officiate after arrival at the venue.

While still in revolutionary mood, a further improvement

would lend a more realistic adherence to a true 40:60 ratio between figures and free-skating. At present, a good free-skater can get 5·8 and 5·9 and even an occasional 6, but the best figures seen, such as Trixi Schuba used to trace, will seldom get more than 5·2.

Until the world's best figure skaters are marked at least 5·7 for their main achievements, the constantly higher average free-skating marks will continue to make nonsense of 40:60.

If a different ratio is desirable, like 70:30 in favour of free-skating, then the rules can be changed to allow for this. But do let a good figure have a high mark, comparable to that given for a good free-skating performance. What ratio is agreed should show in practice as well as in theory.

G

19. Speed Skating

Many people take up skating solely with a view to the racing side of the sport, which I think must inevitably expand a lot as more mechanically frozen outdoor circuits come into being. More costly to maintain than indoor rinks, covering a much larger area, it is not surprising that they are relatively few in number. Indoor speed skating is a poor second best because of the restricted space, so the world's leading ice racers still come mainly from nations climatically suited to natural ice, notably in Northern Europe.

Those who do not live in such latitudes inevitably must first learn at conventional indoor rinks which, apart from the area limitations, provide insufficient straight lengths for adequate speeds and the bends are too sharp and frequent. Indoor rink managements usually can allocate only infrequent periods of ice time for speed skaters.

Budding racers also experience difficulty at these rinks when wishing to practice with other skaters during normal public sessions. Many managements will not permit the use of speed skates at such sessions because abuse of the privilege can be dangerous to the recreational skaters of all grades using the ice at the same time.

The speed skate is appreciably longer than the figure skate. The steel blade is very thin, ideally about one thirty-second of an inch. It is straight, usually twelve to eighteen inches long and designed to travel in straight or nearly straight lines. The boot has much lower heel supports than that used for figures and looks more like a shoe.

In the long term, there is only one way for a racer to make the top grade. Every year, he must spend at least two months in countries which can provide good tracks as well as enough ice. This means that many racers need to travel long distances to get suitable training. Norway is particularly well provided and speed skating in that country commands a spectator following comparable to that of football in other lands.

Leading international 400 metres circuits have been established at Cortina d'Ampezzo, Italy; Davos, Switzerland; Deventer and Heerenveen, Holland; Gothenburg, Sweden; Grenoble, France; Helsinki, Finland; Innsbruck, Austria; Inzell, West Germany; Medeo, USSR; Oslo, Norway; Sapporo, Japan; and West Allis, USA.

Ice speed skating record-holders are the fastest self-propelled humans over level terrain. Ice racers have averaged nearly thirty miles per hour in the shortest races. Over a mile, the speed skater has been approximately one minute faster than the athletics track runner. In 1972 Olympic events, the fastest track athlete over 10 000 metres was more than $12\frac{1}{2}$ seconds slower than the best time achieved on ice over the same distance.

Good ice conditions are not the only ideal to seek in training. The thinner air at high altitudes is another aid to performance. It is no coincidence that most world records have been set on mountain rinks situated higher than 500 metres (1640 ft).

The time of each competitor being the factor deciding results, international championship competitors race only in pairs and in separate lanes, but pack-style racing has been prevalent in the United States.

The comparatively short indoor rinks, giving twelve or sixteen laps to the mile, on which most American, British and other racers have to learn, can develop bad habits in technique. The way in which the blade strikes the ice is very important. The toe is pointed almost straight down in sprints, to get more ride out of the blade.

For distance races the blade is placed on the ice at a forward angle around ten degrees, with the upper body following. The

A/796.91

upper body relaxes above the leg over which it glides. So, when the skater pushes off his right skate he should 'collapse' his upper body over his left thigh. The angle of the legs should be almost straight to the ice – and the straighter line one skates the better it is. The average length of a champion's stroke along the straight is a little under nine yards.

International championship meetings are normally of two days' duration, the usual practice being to stage two of the four events on each day. The best all-round performer over these four distances, calculated on a points basis, is hailed as the overall individual champion (except in the Winter Olympics). So although, as in running, a speed skater soon becomes recognized as primarily either a sprinter or a distance performer, in international events an individual champion on the ice is still determined by his overall ability over the four recognized championship distances, perhaps an outdated tradition when considering that the longest, 10 000 metres, is twenty times as far as the shortest, 500 metres.

On outdoor ice, the stars in action certainly present a thrilling spectacle. Over the longer distances the skater often races with his hands clasped behind his back to conserve energy, making his labour look much more effortless than it is. Each gliding stroke commences on the outside edge of the blade and is rolled over to the inside edge by the end of the stride, a style which dictates an impressive body-roll quite fascinating to watch.

Clad in woollen tights, sweater and protective headgear, these racers – their slightly bent shadows often grotesquely magnified in the reflected light – take the bends with consummate artistry. It is highly exhilarating, affording a dramatic sensation that it is not the skater but the ice beneath him that is moving.

While outdoor ice racing often attracts very large crowds, particularly in Norway and Holland, the sport indoors has remained basically a participants' preoccupation, perhaps partly because of the confusion to spectators when, because of the necessarily small circuit, competitors are frequently lapped.

Ice speed skating began to evolve on the canals of Holland from the middle of the thirteenth century. Some kind of competition took place as early as 1676. Among pioneering Dutch events, the first known women's competition, with an entry of 130, was organized in 1805 on a straight course at Leeuwarden. Notable early men's straight course races were held at Woutdsend in 1823, Dokkum in 1840 and Amsterdam in 1864. After this, tracks became 'U'-shaped, with one sharp bend and an overall length of 160–200 metres (175–220 yd).

During the early nineteenth century, with racing then more usually organized on a two-at-a-time basis, the Dutch took the sport to their closest neighbours, Germany, France and Austria. The Frieslanders of North Holland introduced it to England in the area extending from Cambridge to the Wash known as the Fens, where recorded competitions date from 1814.

A Handbook of Fen Skating, published in London in 1882, contained a drawing of a speed skating contest at Chatteris in 1823, watched by top-hatted spectators in a passing horse-drawn stagecoach. Outstanding British professional skaters of the nineteenth century were William and George Smart, champions from 1854 to 1864 and from 1879 to 1889 respectively. The formation of the National Skating Association of Great Britain in 1879 led to an organized distinction between professionals and amateurs. British amateur championships, over one and a half miles, began at the Welsh Harp, Hendon, in 1800.

Some 10000 spectators watched the first recorded competition in Norway in 1863. The first in Sweden took place in 1882, in Finland in 1883 and in Russia the following year. The sport also spread to North America in the mid-1800s and the earliest outstanding US racer was Tim Donoghue, from 1863 to 1875. The first US championships were staged in 1879 and Joseph Donoghue was a particularly prominent performer in the 1890s. Norwegians who did much to popularize speed skating internationally around this time were Axel Paulsen, Harald Hagen and Carl Werner.

The first international speed skating competition was in Hamburg in 1885, but world championships were not officially recognized until 1893, the year after the International Skating Union was formed.

Men's speed progress in 80 years

1974 world records

Distance (m)	Time	Holder		Venue	Date	Record in 1894	Progress in 80 years
500	38·0	Leo Linkovesi	(Finland)	Davos	8.1.72	47·0	9·0
	38·0	Erhard Keller	(West Germany)	Inzell	4.3.72		
	38·0	Hasse Börjes	(Sweden)	Inzell	4.3.72		
	38·0	Lasse Efskind	(Norway)	Davos	13.1.73		
1500	1:58·7	Ard Schenk	(Netherlands)	Davos	16.1.71	2:28·8	3·01
5000	7: 9·8	Ard Schenk	(Netherlands)	Inzell	4.3.72	8:37·6	1:27·8
10000	14:55·9	Ard Schenk	(Netherlands)	Inzell	14.3.71	19:12·4	4:16·5

Women's speed progress in 40 years

1974 world records

Distance (m)	Time	Holder		Venue	Date	Record in 1934	Progress in 40 years
500	41·8	Sheila Young	(USA)	Davos	19.1.73	50·3	8·5
1000	1:26·4	Tatyana Averina	(USSR)	Medeo,	1.4.74	1:45·7	19·3
1500	2:14·0	Tatayna Averina	(USSR)	Medeo,	2.4.74	2:40·4	26·0
3000	4:46·5	Stien Kaiser	(Netherlands)	Davos	16.1.71	6:52·8	2: 6·3

20. The Fastest Team Game

Twelve heavily padded skaters outwitting and outstriding each other in the world's fastest team game. Some of the speediest self-propelled humans deftly scoring goals with shots sometimes too rapid for the eye to follow. Robust clashing of bodies, flashy stickhandling skill and the skating ability to turn on a sixpence. All at an exciting, temper-testing pace demanding frantic inter-changing with substitutes every few minutes. This is thrill-a-second ice hockey, with every moment of actual play electrically timed – a tough, uncompromising man's game which repeatedly pulls spectators forward in their seats.

The playing area

Ice hockey is a six-a-side game played by skaters with sticks and a rubber puck on a rink measuring, ideally, 200 feet (61 m) long and 85 feet (26 m) wide. Barrier boards which surround the rink are curved at each of the four corners and must be between 4 feet (1·22 m) high and 6 feet (1·83 m) wide, with nets not less than 2 feet (60 cm) deep at the base.

Two blue lines divide the rink equally into three zones, and a centre red line is equidistant between them. The centre of the rink is marked by a blue spot surrounded by a blue circle of 15 feet (4·5 m) radius.

Four red spots in similar sized red circles, two in each half, are marked 15 feet (4·5 m) out from the goal lines, midway between each goal post and barrier. Each side of these four face-off spots are red lines 2 feet (60 cm) long, parallel to the goal lines. Other red lines, 3 feet (90 cm) long, extend from each outer edge of the four red circles. There are two red spots in the centre zone, 5 feet (1·5 cm) from each blue line and midway between the side barriers. Creases in front of each goal are indicated by 6 feet (1·8 m) radius semicircles (IIHF rules) or 8 feet × 4 feet (2·5 m × 1·25 m) rectangles (NHL rules).

How it is played

Amateur matches are controlled by two referees, one for each half of the playing area, but in professional NHL matches one referee is in complete charge, assisted by two linesmen whose main duty is to whistle off-sides.

A game is divided into three periods, each of twenty minutes' actual playing time, measured by stopwatch only while the puck is in play. Although only six players from each team are allowed on the ice at the same time – the normal line-up being the goal-minder, two defencemen and three forwards – substitutes are considered essential because of the fast, energy-sapping speed at which the game is played. A team usually carries between eleven and eighteen players. Substitutes may be introduced at any time.

Play is commenced at the beginning of each period, and after a goal has been scored, by a face-off. The puck is dropped by the referee in the centre of the rink between the sticks of the opposing centremen. Play is restarted at other times of the game by a face-off on the nearest of the other marked spots to the point at which a misplay occurred. The puck becomes dead only when hit over the barrier or when the whistle blows for an infringement.

Goal judges signify a score by switching on a red light behind the goal concerned. A goal can be scored only by propelling the puck from the stick, not by kicking or throwing, nor when an attacking player is in the goal-crease.

The two blue lines divide the playing area into three zones – defence, neutral (centre) and attacking zones. Only three players may be in their own defence zone when the puck is outside it. A

12. Karen Magnussen, Canada's world champion, 1973.

13. Glyn Watts and Hilary Green, Britain's world ice dance runners-up, 1974.

14. *Left:* Val and Sandra Bezic, Canadian pair champions, 1970–4.

15. *Right:* Barry and Louise Soper, Canadian ice dance champions, 1971–4.

16–19. Donald Jackson, Canada's world champion, 1962. Jean Scott, Britain's European runner-up, 1973. Peggy Fleming (USA), thrice world champion, 1966–8, and Olympic gold medallist, 1968. Bernard Ford and Diane Towler, four times world ice dance champions for Britain, 1966–9.

20. A blade for every grade. These highly specialized M K figure skates are designed to suit everyone's individual needs.

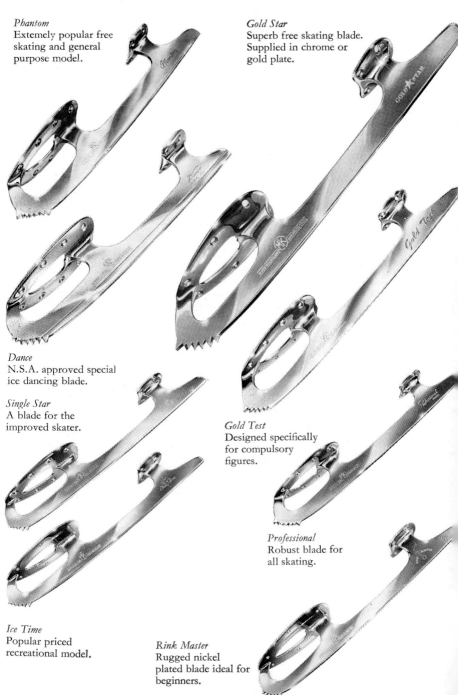

Phantom
Extemely popular free skating and general purpose model.

Gold Star
Superb free skating blade. Supplied in chrome or gold plate.

Dance
N.S.A. approved special ice dancing blade.

Single Star
A blade for the improved skater.

Gold Test
Designed specifically for compulsory figures.

Professional
Robust blade for all skating.

Ice Time
Popular priced recreational model.

Rink Master
Rugged nickel plated blade ideal for beginners.

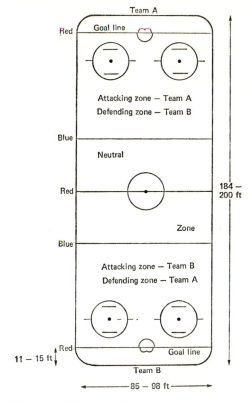

Figure 16. Diagram of an ice hockey rink.

player may only enter the attacking zone in line with or behind the puck or puck-possessor. He may not take a pass from a team-mate who is, at the moment of passing, in another zone. To stay on-side, a player can only pass to a colleague in the same zone (also to anyone in his own half if he is in his defence zone).

Because of the pace and frantic action involved, players are penalized by being sent off the ice for two or more minutes, according to the severity of the offence. The term of the suspension is served in a penalty box, colloquially known as the 'sin bin'. Minor penalties of two minutes are imposed for charging, elbowing, tripping, body-checking, high sticks or deliberately shooting

Penalties

Referee's Signals

CROSSCHECKING

CROSS CHECKING
Referee does series of forward and backward motions with both fists clenched extending from the chest

HIGH STICKING

HIGH STICKING
Referee holds both fists clenched, one above the other, at height of his forehead

BUTT END

BUTT END
Referee makes a cross motion of the forearms, one moving under the other

HOLDING

HOLDING
Referee clasps either wrist with the other hand well in front of body

Figure 17. Signals.

Penalties   Referee's Signals

ELBOWING
Referee taps
either elbow
with the
opposite hand

ELBOWING

TRIPPING
Referee
extending right
leg forward,
clear of ice
strikes it with
right hand
below knee

TRIPPING

HOOKING
Referee makes
series of
tugging motions
with both hands

HOOKING

SPEARING
Referee makes
jabbing motion
with both hands
thrust out
immediately in
front of the body,
and then drops
hands to the side
of the body.

SPEARING

out of the rink. A goalminder's minor penalty is served by a team colleague. More severe penalties of five or ten minutes, or for the remainder of the game, are imposed according to the seriousness of the offence.

Equipment

Sticks, made entirely of wood, are limited to 53 inches (135 cm) handle and 14½ inches (37 cm) blade, except in the case of the

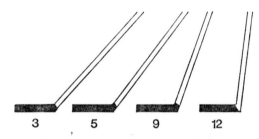

3   5   9   12

Figure 18. Blade lies of an ice hockey stick. Most players favour a 5 or 6 lie. Goalminders use 11, 12 or 13. The higher the lie, the closer the puck is carried to the skater.

goalminder, who may use a heavier and wider stick. The angle (lie) between the blade and handle varies and blades are shaped to a player's individual needs.

Boots have lower ankle supports than those used for figure skating, coming up only 4–5 inches (10–12 cm) above the sole. Important features are the reinforced caps at toe and heel, moulded arch supports and tendon protectors.

The ice hockey skate blade is shorter than the speed skate and only a sixteenth of an inch (1·5 mm) wide. The blade is reinforced with hollow tubing for greater strength and lighter weight. The goalminder's more specialized skate is wider and less high, affording easier balance. Extra stanchions are fitted to prevent the puck from passing underneath his boots.

The puck is circular, made of solid vulcanized rubber, 3 inches

(7·6 cm) in diameter, 1 inch (2·5 cm) thick, and weighs about 5½ ounces (156 g).

Apparel is highly specialized to cater for the sport's protective needs. All the players wear knee-pads, shin-guards, elbow-pads, shoulder-guards, thick gauntlet-type gloves, long stockings that fit over the knee-pads, and a special type of shorts with sweaters in team colours to complete the outfit.

Helmets, though optional, are a wise precaution to minimize possible head injuries. For special protection, the goalminder wears extra large leather leg-guards, a chest protector and extra-padded gloves (a different type of glove for holding the stick to the one for the catching hand). Some goalies also wear a face-mask to avoid possible cuts from skates or sticks after falling on the ice.

How the sport evolved

The game's historical roots are deeply embedded in Canadian ice, stemming from a game played by Englishmen on the frozen expanse of Kingston Harbour, Ontario, in 1860. This, the first time a puck was used instead of a ball, clearly separated the game's identity from field hockey. The pioneer players were mainly Crimean War veterans in a Royal Canadian Rifles regiment. Montreal subsequently became the central point of the game's early progress.

In 1879, two Montreal students at McGill University, W. F. Robertson and R. F. Smith, devised the first rules by adding a few original ideas to what was basically a combination of field hockey and Rugby football regulations. A square puck was used, with nine players on each side, and this led to the formation of the first recognized team, McGill University Hockey Club, in 1880.

Leagues of all grades thrived throughout Canada, with nearly a hundred clubs in Montreal alone, before the game was first played in the United States in 1893 – by Yale University in New Haven and John Hopkins University in Baltimore. That same year, Lord Stanley of Preston, then Governor-General of Canada, donated the Stanley Cup as a permanent senior trophy which was destined to become the sport's most famous prize. It was first won in 1894 on natural ice by a team representing Montreal Amateur Athletic Association.

The US Amateur Hockey League was founded in New York City in 1896 and the sport began to grow in Europe at the turn of the century. The International Ice Hockey Federation was formed in 1908, with Belgium, Bohemia, France, Great Britain and Switzerland its founder members.

Canadian demonstration popularized the game in Great Britain sufficiently to inspire a five-team league competition in 1903. The first game in Scotland took place at Crossmyloof, Glasgow, in 1908. The first European championship was won by Great Britain in 1910 at Les Avants, in the Swiss Alps. The British Ice Hockey Association was not founded until 1914.

The world's major professional competition, the National Hockey League of North America, has been contested between the foremost clubs in the United States and Canada and was inaugurated at Montreal in 1917. From 1943, the League settled to a regular contest between what are now the world's six most famous teams – Boston Bruins, Chicago Black Hawks, Detroit Red Wings, Montreal Canadiens, New York Rangers and Toronto Maple Leafs. In 1967 the League was doubled in size to twelve clubs and divided into two divisions. Other teams have since been added and a rival North American league of twelve clubs in two divisions began in 1971 under the grandiose and somewhat misleading title of World Hockey Association.

At the end of the NHL matches, the top four in each division compete in two separate play-off series, the winner of each finally meeting in a best-of-seven-matches contest for the Stanley Cup, now emblematic of North American ice hockey supremacy. It has been held most times by Montreal Canadiens, whose 1973 victory was their eighteenth.

Britain's best years date from 1934, when the Empire Pool, Wembley, came into being, two years before Britain became Olympic champions. The Second World War rudely curtailed this promising forward surge, and teams and talent in Britain, afterwards faced with an acute shortage of large ice arenas with worthwhile spectator accommodation, faded frustratingly while ice hockey expanded wherever else it was played.

An important British revival was spearheaded at Wembley in 1973 by the formation of a new, North American-owned club, the London Lions, which, with imported players of top world-class, inspired the formation of a European League that the organizers hope will eventually rank on a par with the NHL.

There are now thousands of teams throughout North America taking part in league competitions comparable in diversity to those of soccer in Britain. The Allan Cup in Canada, first contested in 1908, is widely regarded as the game's most coveted amateur club trophy.

By the 1970s the approximate number of players registered in the Soviet Union was 300000; Canada 250000; Sweden 140000; Czechoslovakia 77000; and Finland 40000. Outside Europe and North America, the sport has grown in proportion to the limited ice acreage available in such warmer-climate countries as Australia, Japan and South Africa.

21. World Championships

The International Skating Union having been founded in 1892, ice skating was one of the earliest sports to be competitively well organized on a worldwide basis.

World speed skating championships for men were first officially recognized in 1893, when the Dutch skater, Jaap Eden, became the first winner. The first women's world championship was contested at Stockholm in 1936 and won by Kit Klein of the United States.

World speed titles have been accorded always to the overall best performers in events over four distances and not to winners of individual events. The title is calculated on a points basis and so it is possible for a consistently high placed racer to become world champion without winning any of the individual events.

The men's distances now raced are 500, 1500 5000 and 10 000 metres. The women's distances are 500, 1000 3000 and 5000 metres. The most successful men's champions have been the Norwegian, Oscar Mathisen, and the Finn, Clas Thunberg, who each won five times. The outstanding woman has been the Russian, Inga Artamonova, with four wins.

The first world championship in figure skating, at St Petersburg (Leningrad) in 1896, was won by a German, Dr. Gilbert Fuchs. Women, who at first had been allowed to compete with the men, began separate championships ten years later, when Madge Syers won for Great Britain in 1906 (previously having been runner-up in the men's event in 1902). In 1908, the Germans,

Heinrich Burger and Anna Hübler, took the first world pair skating title at St Petersburg (Leningrad).

Ulrich Salchow of Sweden has won the men's title a record ten times, in two straight runs of five. Norway's Sonja Henie, with ten consecutive victories, has been the outstanding woman. The most successful pairs have been the Russians, Oleg Protopopov with Ludmila Belousova and Alexsei Ulanov with Irina Rodnina, each gaining four successive wins. In 1952, Paris staged the first officially recognized world ice dance championship, one of four straight wins by Lawrence Demmy and Jean Westwood of Britain. This run has been thrice equalled – by the Czechs, Pavel Roman and Eva Romanova; by another British couple, Bernard Ford and Diane Towler; and by the Russians, Aleksandr Gorshkov and Ludmila Pakhomova, who went on to a record fifth triumph in 1974.

The first world championship in ice hockey was won by Canada at Antwerp in 1920. The first three titles were decided quadrennially and concurrently with the Olympics, but contests have been held annually from 1930, except for wartime interruption. The Olympic titles continued to be decided concurrently every fourth year until 1972, when a separate world championship was held. Canada has won the championship most times – nineteen in all – but from 1970 has not participated because of a disagreement concerning the question of including professionals.

World championship tournaments in latter years have been divided into three groups of six or more teams, which play each other in their group on a league points basis. The top team in Group A takes the world title. Interest in the other groups is boosted by the annual promotion and relegation of top and bottom teams.

H

World Figure Skating Championships
Men

	Gold	Silver	Bronze
1896 Leningrad	Gilbert Fuchs (Germany)	Gustav Hügel (Austria)	Georg Sanders (Russia)
1897 Stockholm	Gustav Hügel (Austria)	Ulrich Salchow (Sweden)	Johan Lefstad (Norway)
1898 London	Henning Grenander (Sweden)	Gustav Hügel (Austria)	Gilbert Fuchs (Germany)
1899 Davos	Gustav Hügel (Austria)	Ulrich Salchow (Sweden)	Edgar Syers (Great Britain)
1900 Davos	Gustav Hügel (Austria)	Ulrich Salchow (Sweden)	
1901 Stockholm	Ulrich Salchow (Sweden)	Gilbert Fuchs (Germany)	
1902 London	Ulrich Salchow (Sweden)	Madge Syers (Great Britain)	Martin Gordan (Germany)
1903 Leningrad	Ulrich Salchow (Sweden)	Nicolai Panin (Russia)	Max Bohatsch (Austria)
1904 Berlin	Ulrich Salchow (Sweden)	Heinrich Burger (Germany)	Martin Gordan (Germany)
1905 Stockholm	Ulrich Salchow (Sweden)	Max Bohatsch (Austria)	Per Thorén (Sweden)
1906 Munich	Gilbert Fuchs (Germany)	Heinrich Burger (Germany)	Bror Meyer (Sweden)
1907 Vienna	Ulrich Salchow (Sweden)	Max Bohatsch (Austria)	Gilbert Fuchs (Germany)
1908 Troppau	Ulrich Salchow (Sweden)	Gilbert Fuchs (Germany)	Heinrich Burger (Germany)
1909 Stockholm	Ulrich Salchow (Sweden)	Per Thorén (Sweden)	Ernest Herz (Austria)
1910 Davos	Ulrich Salchow (Sweden)	Werner Rittberger (Germany)	Andor Szende (Hungary)
1911 Berlin	Ulrich Salchow (Sweden)	Werner Rittberger (Germany)	Fritz Kachler (Austria)
1912 Manchester	Fritz Kachler (Austria)	Werner Rittberger (Germany)	Andor Szende (Hungary)
1913 Vienna	Fritz Kachler (Austria)	Willy Böckl (Austria)	Andor Szende (Hungary)

	Gold	Silver	Bronze
1914 Helsinki	Gösta Sandahl (Sweden)	Fritz Kachler (Austria)	Willy Böckl (Austria)
1922 Stockholm	Gillis Grafström (Sweden)	Fritz Kachler (Austria)	Willy Böckl (Austria)
1923 Vienna	Fritz Kachler (Austria)	Willy Böckl (Austria)	Gösta Sandahl (Sweden)
1924 Manchester	Gillis Grafström (Sweden)	Willy Böckl (Austria)	Ernst Oppacher (Austria)
1925 Vienna	Willy Böckl (Austria)	Fritz Kachler (Austria)	Otto Preissecker (Austria)
1926 Berlin	Willy Böckl (Austria)	Otto Preissecker (Austria)	John Page (Great Britain)
1927 Davos	Willy Böckl (Austria)	Otto Preissecker (Austria)	Karl Schäfer (Austria)
1928 Berlin	Willy Böckl (Austria)	Karl Schäfer (Austria)	Hugo Distler (Austria)
1929 London	Gillis Grafström (Sweden)	Karl Schäfer (Austria)	Ludwig Wrede (Austria)
1930 New York	Karl Schäfer (Austria)	Roger Turner (USA)	Georg Gautschi (Switzerland)
1931 Berlin	Karl Schäfer (Austria)	Roger Turner (USA)	Ernst Baier (Germany)
1932 Montreal	Karl Schäfer (Austria)	Mongomery Wilson (Canada)	Ernst Baier (Germany)
1933 Zürich	Karl Schäfer (Austria)	Ernst Baier (Germany)	Markus Nikkanen (Finland)
1934 Stockholm	Karl Schäfer (Austria)	Ernst Baier (Germany)	Erich Erdös (Austria)
1935 Budapest	Karl Schäfer (Austria)	Jack Dunn (Great Britain)	Dénes Pataky (Hungary)
1936 Paris	Karl Schäfer (Austria)	Graham Sharp (Great Britain)	Felix Kaspar (Austria)
1937 Vienna	Felix Kaspar (Austria)	Graham Sharp (Great Britain)	Elemér Tertak (Hungary)
1938 Berlin	Felix Kaspar (Austria)	Graham Sharp (Great Britain)	Herbert Alward (Austria)
1939 Budapest	Graham Sharp (Great Britain)	Freddie Tomlins (Great Britain)	Horst Faber (Germany)
1947 Stockholm	Hans Gerschwiler (Switzerland)	Dick Button (USA)	Arthur Apfel (Great Britain)

	Gold	*Silver*	*Bronze*
1948 Davos	Dick Button (USA)	Hans Gerschwiler (Switzerland)	Ede Kiraly (Hungary)
1949 Paris	Dick Button (USA)	Ede Király (Hungary)	Edi Rada (Austria)
1950 London	Dick Button (USA)	Ede Király (Hungary)	Hayes Jenkins (USA)
1951 Milan	Dick Button (USA)	James Grogan (USA)	Helmut Seibt (Austria)
1952 Paris	Dick Button (USA)	James Grogan (USA)	Hayes Jenkins (USA)
1953 Davos	Hayes Jenkins (USA)	James Grogan (USA)	Carlo Fassi (Italy)
1954 Oslo	Hayes Jenkins (USA)	James Grogan (USA)	Alain Giletti (France)
1955 Vienna	Hayes Jenkins (USA)	Ronald Robertson (USA)	David Jenkins (USA)
1956 Garmisch	Hayes Jenkins (USA)	Ronald Robertson (USA)	David Jenkins (USA)
1957 Colorado Springs	David Jenkins (USA)	Tim Brown (USA)	Charles Snelling (Canada)
1958 Paris	David Jenkins (USA)	Tim Brown (USA)	Alain Giletti (France)
1959 Colorado Springs	David Jenkins (USA)	Donald Jackson (Canada)	Tim Brown (USA)
1960 Vancouver	Alain Giletti (France)	Donald Jackson (Canada)	Alain Calmat (France)
1962 Prague	Donald Jackson (Canada)	Carol Divin (Czechoslovakia)	Alain Calmat (France)
1963 Cortina	Donald McPherson (Canada)	Alain Calmat (France)	Manfred Schnelldorfer (West Germany)
1964 Dortmund	Manfred Schnelldorfer (West Germany)	Alain Calmat (France)	Carol Divin (Czechoslovakia)
1965 Colorado Springs	Alain Calmat (France)	Scott Allen (USA)	Donald Knight (Canada)
1966 Davos	Emmerich Danzer (Austria)	Wolfgang Schwarz (Austria)	Gary Visconti (USA)
1967 Vienna	Emmerich Danzer (Austria)	Wolfgang Schwarz (Austria)	Gary Visconti (USA)

	Gold	*Silver*	*Bronze*
1968 Geneva	Emmerich Danzer (Austria)	Tim Wood (USA)	Patrick Pera (France)
1969 Colorado Springs	Tim Wood (USA)	Ondrej Nepela (Czechoslovakia)	Patrick Pera (France)
1970 Ljubljana	Tim Wood (USA)	Ondrej Nepela (Czechoslovakia)	Gunter Zöller (East Germany)
1971 Lyon	Ondrej Nepela (Czechoslovakia)	Patrick Pera (France)	Sergei Chetverukhin (USSR)
1972 Calgary	Ondrej Nepela (Czechoslovakia)	Sergei Chetverukhin (USSR)	Vladimir Kovalev (USSR)
1973 Bratislava	Ondrej Nepela (Czechoslovakia)	Sergei Chetverukhin (USSR)	Jan Hoffmann (East Germany)
1974 Munich	Jan Hoffmann (East Germany)	Sergei Volkov (USSR)	Toller Cranston (Canada)

Women

	Gold	*Silver*	*Bronze*
1906 Davos	Madge Syers (Great Britain)	Jenny Herz (Austria)	Lily Kronberger (Hungary)
1907 Vienna	Madge Syers (Great Britain)	Jenny Herz (Austria)	Lily Kronberger (Hungary)
1908 Troppau	Lily Kronberger (Hungary)	Elsa Rendschmidt (Germany)	
1909 Budapest	Lily Kronberger (Hungary)		
1910 Berlin	Lily Kronberger (Hungary)	Elsa Rendschmidt (Germany)	
1911 Vienna	Lily Kronberger (Hungary)	Opika von Horvath (Hungary)	Ludowika Eilers (Germany)
1912 Davos	Opika von Horvath (Hungary)	Grennhough Smith (Great Britain)	Phyllis Johnson (Great Britain)
1913 Stockholm	Opika von Horvath (Hungary)	Phyllis Johnson (Great Britain)	Svea Norén (Sweden)
1914 St Moritz	Opika von Horvath (Hungary)	Angela Hanka (Austria)	Phyllis Johnson (Great Britain)
1922 Stockholm	Herma Plank-Szabo (Austria)	Svea Norén (Sweden)	Margot Moe (Norway)
1923 Vienna	Herma Plank-Szabo (Austria)	Gisela Reichmann (Austria)	Svea Norén (Sweden)

	Gold	Silver	Bronze
1924 Oslo	Herma Plank-Szabo (Austria)	Ellen Brockhöfft (Germany)	Beatrix Loughran (USA)
1925 Davos	Herma Jaross-Szabo (Austria)	Ellen Brockhöfft (Germany)	Elisabeth Böckel (Germany)
1926 Stockholm	Herma Jaross-Szabo (Austria))	Sonja Henie (Norway)	Kathleen Shaw (Great Britain)
1927 Oslo	Sonja Henie (Norway)	Herma Jarozss-Sabo (Austria)	Karen Simensen (Norway)
1928 London	Sonja Henie (Norway)	Maribel Vinson (USA)	Fritzi Burger (Austria)
1929 Budapest	Sonja Henie (Norway)	Fritzi Burger (Austria)	Melitta Brunner (Austria)
1930 New York	Sonja Henie (Norway)	Cecil Smith (Canada)	Maribel Vinson (USA)
1931 Berlin	Sonja Henie (Norway)	Hilde Holovsky (Austria)	Fritzi Burger (Austria)
1932 Montreal	Sonja Henie (Norway)	Fritzi Burger (Austria)	Constance Samuel (Canada)
1933 Stockholm	Sonja Henie (Norway)	Vivi-Anne Hultén (Sweden)	Hilde Holovsky (Austria)
1934 Oslo	Sonja Henie (Norway)	Megan Taylor (Great Britain)	Liselotte Landbeck (Austria)
1935 Vienna	Sonja Henie (Norway)	Cecilia Colledge (Great Britain)	Vivi-Anne Hultén (Sweden)
1936 Paris	Sonja Henie (Norway)	Megan Taylor (Great Britain)	Vivi-Anne Hultén (Sweden)
1937 London	Cecilia Colledge (Great Britain)	Megan Taylor (Great Britain)	Vivi-Anne Hultén (Sweden)
1938 Stockholm	Megan Taylor (Great Britain)	Cecilia Colledge (Great Britain)	Hedy Stenuf (USA)
1939 Prague	Megan Taylor (Great Britain)	Hedy Stenuf (USA)	Daphne Walker (Great Britain)
1947 Stockholm	Barbara Ann Scott (Canada)	Daphne Walker (Great Britain)	Gretchen Merrill (USA)
1948 Davos	Barbara Ann Scott (Canada)	Eva Pawlik (Austria)	Jirina Nekolova (Czechoslovakia)
1949 Paris	Aja Vrzanova (Czechoslovakia)	Yvonne Sherman (USA)	Jeannette Altwegg (Great Britain)
1950 London	Aja Vrzanova (Czechoslovakia)	Jeannette Altwegg (Great Britain)	Yvonne Sherman (USA)

	Gold	Silver	Bronze
1951 Milan	Jeannette Altwegg (Great Britain)	Jacqueline du Bief (France)	Sonya Klopfer (USA)
1952 Paris	Jacqueline du Bief (France)	Sonya Klopfer (USA)	Virginia Baxter (USA)
1953 Davos	Tenley Albright (USA)	Gundi Busch (Germany)	Valda Osborn (Great Britain)
1954 Oslo	Gundi Busch (Germany)	Tenley Albright (USA)	Erica Batchelor (Great Britain)
1955 Vienna	Tenley Albright (USA)	Carol Heiss (USA)	Hanna Eigel (Austria)
1956 Garmisch	Carol Heiss (USA)	Tenley Albright (USA)	Ingrid Wendl (Austria)
1957 Colorado Springs	Carol Heiss (USA)	Hanna Eigel (Austria)	Ingrid Wendl (Austria)
1958 Paris	Carol Heiss (USA)	Ingrid Wendl (Austria)	Hanna Walter (Austria)
1959 Colorado Springs	Carol Heiss (USA)	Hanna Walter (Austria)	Sjoukje Dijkstra (Netherlands)
1960 Vancouver	Carol Heiss (USA)	Sjoukje Dijkstra (Netherlands)	Barbara Roles (USA)
1962 Prague	Sjoukje Dijkstra (Netherlands)	Wendy Griner (Canada)	Regine Heitzer (Austria)
1963 Cortina	Sjoukje Dijkstra (Netherlands)	Regine Heitzer (Austria)	Nicole Hassler (France)
1964 Dortmund	Sjoukje Dijkstra (Netherlands)	Regine Heitzer (Austria)	Petra Burka (Canada)
1965 Colorado Springs	Petra Burka (Canada)	Regine Heitzer (Austria)	Peggy Fleming (USA)
1966 Davos	Peggy Fleming (USA)	Gabriele Seyfert (East Germany)	Petra Burka (Canada)
1967 Vienna	Peggy Fleming (USA)	Gabriele Seyfert (East Germany)	Hana Maskova (Czechoslovakia)
1968 Geneva	Peggy Fleming (USA)	Gabriele Seyfert (East Germany)	Hana Maskova (Czechoslovakia)
1969 Colorado Springs	Gabriele Seyfert (East Germany)	Beatrix Schuba (Austria)	Zsuzsa Almassy (Hungary)
1970 Ljubljana	Garbiele Seyfert (East Germany)	Beatrix Schuba (Austria)	Julie Holmes (USA)
1971 Lyon	Beatrix Schuba (Austria)	Julie Holmes (USA)	Karen Magnussen (Canada)

	Gold	Silver	Bronze
1972 Calgary	Beatrix Schuba (Austria)	Karen Magnussen (Canada)	Janet Lynn (USA)
1973 Bratislava	Karen Magnussen (Canada)	Janet Lynn (USA)	Christine Errath (East Germany)
1974 Munich	Christine Errath (East Germany)	Dorothy Hamill (USA)	Dianne de Leeuw (Netherlands)

Pairs

	Gold	Silver	Bronze
1908 Leningrad	Heinrich Burger Anna Hübler (Germany)	James Johnson Phyllis Johnson (Great Britain)	L. Popowa A. Fischer (Russia)
1909 Stockholm	James Johnson Phyllis Johnson (Great Britain)	Nils Rosenius Valborg Lindahl (Sweden)	Richard Johanson Gertrud Ström (Sweden)
1910 Berlin	Heinrich Burger Anna Hübler (Germany)	Walter Jakobsson Ludowika Eilers (Finland)	James Johnson Phyllis Johnson (Great Britain)
1911 Vienna	Walter Jakobsson Ludowika Eilers (Finland)		
1912 Manchester	James Johnson Phyllis Johnson (Great Britain)	Walter Jakobsson Ludowika Eilers (Finland)	Yngvar Bryn Alexia Schöyen (Norway)
1913 Stockholm	Karl Mejstrik Helene Engelmann (Austria)	Walter Jakobsson Ludowika Eilers (Finland)	Leo Horwitz Christa von Szabo (Austria)
1914 St Moritz	Walter Jakobsson Ludowika Eilers (Finland)	Karl Maejstrik Helene Engelmann (Austria)	Leo Horwitz Christa von Szabo (Austria)
1922 Davos	Alfred Berger Helene Engelmann (Austria)	Walter Jakobbson Ludowika Eilers (Finland)	Paul Metzner Margaret Metzner (Germany)
1923 Oslo	Walter Jakobsson Ludowika Eilers (Finland)	Yngvar Bryn Alexia Schöyen (Norway)	Kaj af Ekström Elna Henrikson (Sweden)
1924 Manchester	Alfred Berger Helene Engelmann (Austria)	John Page Ethel Muckelt (Great Britain)	Kaj af Ekström Elna Henrikson (Sweden)

	Gold	*Silver*	*Bronze*
1925 Vienna	Ludwig Wrede Herma Jaross-Szabo (Austria)	Pierre Brunet Andrée Joly (France)	Otto Kaiser Lilly Scholz (Austria)
1926 Berlin	Pierre Brunet Andrée Joly (France)	Otto Kaiser Lilly Scholz (Austria)	Ludwig Wrede Herma Jaross-Szabo (Austria)
1927 Vienna	Ludwig Wrede Herma Jaross-Szabo (Austria)	Otto Kaiser Lilly Scholz (Austria)	Oscar Hoppe Else Hoppe (Czechoslovakia)
1928 London	Pierre Brunet Andrée Joly (France)	Otto Kaiser Lilly Scholz (Austria)	Ludwig Wrede Melitta Brunner (Austria)
1929 Budapest	Otto Kaiser Lilly Scholz (Austria)	Ludwig Wrede Melitta Brunner (Austria)	Sandor Szalay Olga Organista (Hungary)
1930 New York	Pierre Brunet Andrée Joly (France)	Ludwig Wrede Melitta Brunner (Austria)	Sherwin Badger Beatrix Loughran (USA)
1931 Berlin	László Szollás Emilie Rotter (Hungary)	Sandor Szalay Olga Organista (Hungary)	Karl Zwack Idi Papez (Austria)
1932 Montreal	Pierre Brunet Andrée Joly (France)	László Szollás Emilie Rotter (Hungary)	Sherwin Badger Beatrix Loughran (USA)
1933 Stockholm	László Szollás Emilie Rotter (Hungary)	Karl Zwack Idi Papez (Austria)	Chris Christensen Randi Bakke (Norway)
1934 Helsinki	László Szollás Emilie Rotter (Hungary)	Karl Zwack Idi Papez (Austria)	Ernst Baier Maxi Herber (Germany)
1935 Budapest	László Szollás Emilie Rotter (Hungary)	Erich Pausin Ilse Pausin (Austria)	Rezsö Dillinger Lucy Gallo (Hungary)
1936 Paris	Ernst Baier Maxi Herber (Germany)	Erich Pausin Ilse Pausin (Austria)	Leslie Cliff Violet Cliff (Great Britain)
1937 London	Ernst Baier Maxi Herber (Germany)	Erich Pausin Ilse Pausin (Austria)	Leslie Cliff Violet Cliff (Great Britain)
1938 Berlin	Ernst Baier Maxi Herber (Germany)	Erich Pausin Ilse Pausin (Austria)	Günther Noack Inge Koch (Germany)

	Gold	*Silver*	*Bronze*
1939 Budapest	Ernst Baier Maxi Herber (Germany)	Erich Pausin Ilse Pausin (Austria)	Günther Noack Inge Koch (Germany)
1947 Stockholm	Pierre Baugniet Micheline Lennoy (Belgium)	Peter Kennedy Karol Kennedy (USA)	Edmond Verbustel Suzanne Diskeuve (Beglium)
1948 Davos	Pierre Baugniet Micheline Lannoy (Belgium)	Ede Király Andrea Kékesy (Hungary)	Wallace Diestelmeyer Suzanne Morrow (Canada)
1949 Paris	Ede Király Andrea Kékesy (Hungary)	Peter Kennedy Karol Kennedy (USA)	Carleton Hoffner Ann Davies (USA)
1950 London	Peter Kennedy Karol Kennedy (USA)	John Nicks Jennifer Nicks (Great Britain)	Laszlo Nagy Marianne Nagy (Hungary)
1951 Milan	Paul Falk Ria Baran (Germany)	Peter Kennedy Karol Kennedy (USA)	John Nicks Jenniffer Nicks (Great Britain)
1952 Paris	Paul Falk Ria Baran (Germany)	Peter Kennedy Karol Kennedy (USA)	John Nicks Jennifer Nicks (Great Britain)
1953 Davos	John Nicks Jennifer Nicks (Great Britain)	Norris Bowden Frances Dafoe (Canada)	Laszlo Nagy Marianne Nagy (Hungary)
1954 Oslo	Norris Bowden Frances Dafoe (Canada)	Michel Grandjean Silvia Grandjean (Switzerland)	Kurt Oppelt Sissy Schwarz (Austria)
1955 Vienna	Norris Bowden Frances Dafoe (Canada)	Kurt Oppelt Sissy Schwarz (Austria)	Laszlo Nagy Marianne Nagy (Hungary)
1956 Germisch	Kurt Oppelt Sissy Schwarz (Austria)	Norris Bowden Frances Dafoe (Canada)	Franz Ningel Marika Kilius (West Germany)
1957 Colorado Springs	Robert Paul Barbara Wagner (Canada)	Franz Ningel Marika Kilius (West Germany)	Otto Jelinek Maria Jelinek (Canada)
1958 Paris	Robert Paul Barbara Wagner (Canada)	Zdenek Dolezai Vera Suchankova (Czechoslovakia)	Otto Jelinek Maria Jelinek (Canada)
1959 Colorado Springs	Robert Paul Barbara Wagner (Canada)	Hans Bäumler Marika Kilius (West Germany)	Ronald Ludington Nancy Ludington (USA)

	Gold	Silver	Bronze
1960 Vancouver	Robert Paul Barbara Wagner (Canada)	Otto Jelinek Maria Jelinek (Canada)	Hans Bäumler Marika Kilius (West Germany)
1962 Prague	Otto Jelinek Maria Jelinek (Canada)	Oleg Protopopov Ludmila Belousova (USSR)	Franz Ningel Margret Göbl (West Germany)
1963 Cortina	Hans Bäumler Marika Kilius (West Germany)	Oleg Protopopov Ludmila Belousova (USSR)	Alexandr Gavrilov Tatjana Zhuk (USSR)
1964 Dortmund	Hans Bäumler Marika Kilius (West Germany)	Oleg Protopopov Ludmila Belousova (USSR)	Guy Revell Debbi Wilkes (Canada)
1965 Colorado Springs	Oleg Protopopov Ludmila Belousova (USSR)	Ronald Joseph Vivian Joseph (USA)	Alexandr Gorelik Tatjana Zhuk (USSR)
1966 Davos	Oleg Protopopov Ludmila Belousova (USSR)	Alexandr Gorelik Tatjana Zhuk (USSR)	Ronald Kauffman Cynthia Kauffman (USA)
1967 Vienna	Oleg Protopopov Ludmila Belousova (USSR)	Wolfgang Danne Margot Glockshuber (West Germany)	Ronald Kauffman Cynthia Kauffman (USA)
1968 Geneva	Oleg Protopopov Ludmila Belousova (USSR)	Alexandr Gorelik Tatjana Zhuk (USSR)	Ronald Kauffman Cynthia Kauffman (USA)
1969 Colorado Springs	Alexsei Ulanov Irina Rodnina (USSR)	Alexsei Mishin Tamara Moskvina (USSR)	Oleg Protopopov Ludmila Belousova (USSR)
1970 Ljublijana	Alexsei Ulanov Irina Rodnina (USSR)	Andrei Suraikin Ludmila Smirnova (USSR)	Heinz Walther Heidemarie Steiner (East Germany)
1971 Lyon	Alexsei Ulanov Irina Rodnina (USSR)	Andrei Suraikin Ludmila Smirnova (USSR)	Kenneth Shelley Jo Jo Starbuck (USA)
1972 Calgary	Alexsei Ulanov Irina Rodnina (USSR)	Andrei Suraikin Ludmila Smirnova (USSR)	Kenneth Shelley Jo Jo Starbuck (USA)
1973 Bratislava	Alexandr Zaitsev Irina Rodnina (USSR)	Alexsei Ulanov Ludmila Smirnova (USSR)	Uwe Kagelmann Manuela Gross (East Germany)
1974 Munich	Alexandr Zaitsev Irina Rodnina (USSR)	Alexsei Ulanov Ludmila Smirnova (USSR)	Rolf Oesterreich Romy Kermer (East Germany)

Ice Dance

	Gold	Silver	Bronze
1952 Paris	Lawrence Demmy Jean Westwood (Great Britain)	John Slater Joan Dewhirst (Great Britain)	Daniel Ryan Carol Peters (USA)
1953 Davos	Lawrence Demmy Jean Westwood (Great Britain)	John Slater Joan Dewhirst (Great Britain)	Daniel Ryan Carol Peters (USA)
1954 Oslo	Lawrence Demmy Jean Westwood (Great Britain)	Paul Thomas Nesta Davies (Great Britain)	Edward Bodel Carmel Bodel (USA)
1955 Vienna	Lawrence Demmy Jean Westwood (Great Britain)	Paul Thomas Pamela Weight (Great Britain)	Raymond Lockwood Barbara Radford (Great Britain)
1956 Garmisch	Paul Thomas Pamela Weight (Great Britain)	Courtney Jones June Markham (Great Britain)	Gerard Rigby Barbara Thompson (Great Britain)
1957 Colorado Springs	Courtney Jones June Markham (Great Britain)	William McLachlan Géraldine Fenton (Canada)	Bert Wright Sharon McKenzie (USA)
1958 Paris	Courtney Jones June Markham (Great Britain)	William McLachlan Géraldine Fenton (Canada)	Donald Jacoby Andrée Anderson (USA)
1959 Colorado Springs	Courtney Jones Doreen Denny (Great Britain)	Donald Jacoby Andrée Anderson (USA)	William McLachlan Géraldine Fenton (Canada)
1960 Vancouver	Courtney Jones Doreen Denny (Great Britain)	William McLachlan Virginia Thompson (Canada)	Jean-Paul Guhel Christine Guhel (France)
1962 Prague	Pavel Roman Eva Romanova (Czechoslovakia)	Jean-Paul Guhel Christine Guhel (France)	William McLachlan Virginia Thompson (Canada)
1963 Cortina	Pavel Roman Eva Romanova (Czechoslovakia)	Michael Phillips Linda Shearman (Great Britain)	Kenneth Ormsby Paulette Doan (Canada)
1964 Dortmund	Pavel Roman Eva Romanova (Czechoslovakia)	Kenneth Ormsby Paulette Doan (Canada)	David Hickinbottom Janet Sawbridge (Great Britain)
1965 Colorado Springs	Pavel Roman Eva Romanova (Czechoslovakia)	David Hickinbottom Janet Sawbridge (Great Britain)	John Carrell Lorna Dyer (USA)

	Gold	Silver	Bronze
1966 Davos	Bernard Ford Diane Towler (Great Britain)	Dennis Sveum Kristin Fortune (USA)	John Carrell JoLorna Dyer (USA)
1967 Vienna	Bernard Ford Diane Towler (Great Britain)	John Carrell Lorna Dyer (USA)	Malcolm Cannon Yvonne Suddick (Great Britain)
1968 Geneva	Bernard Ford Diane Towler (Great Britain)	Malcolm Cannon Yvonne Suddick (Great Britain)	Jon Lane Janet Sawbridge (Great Britain)
1969 Colorado Springs	Bernard Ford Diane Towler (Great Britain)	Aleksandr Gorshkov Ludmila Pakhomova (USSR)	James Sladky Judy Schwomeyer (USA)
1970 Ljubljana	Aleksandr Gorshkov Ludmila Pakhomova (USSR)	James Sladky Judy Schwomeyer (USA)	Erich Buck Angelika Buck (West Germany)
1971 Lyon	Aleksandr Gorshkov Ludmila Pakhomova (USSR)	Erich Buck Angelika Buck (West Germany)	James Sladky Judy Schwomeyer (USA)
1972 Calgary	Aleksandr Gorshkov Ludmila Pakhomova (USSR)	Erich Buck Angelika Buck (West Germany)	James Sladky Judy Schwomeyer (USA)
1973 Bratislava	Aleksandr Gorshkov Ludmila Pakhomova (USSR)	Erich Buck Angelika Buck (West Germany)	Glyn Watts Hilary Green (Great Britain)
1974 Munich	Aleksandr Gorshkov Ludmila Pakhomova (USSR)	Glyn Watts Hilary Green (Great Britain)	Gennadi Karponosov Natalia Linnichuk (USSR)

Men's World Ice Speed Skating Champions

	500 metres	Time	1500 metres	Time
1893 Amsterdam	Jaap Eden (Netherlands)	51·2	Jaap Eden (Netherlands)	2:48·2
1894 Stockholm	Oscar Fredriksen (Norway)	50·4	Einar Halvorsen (Norway)	2:35·6
1895 Hamar	Oscar Fredriksen (Norway)	48·2	Jaap Eden (Netherlands)	2:25·4
1896 Leningrad	Jaap Eden (Netherlands)	50·2	Jaap Eden (Netherlands)	2:36·2
1897 Montreal	Alfred Naess (Norway)	46·8	Jack McCulloch (Canada)	2:40·8
1898 Davos	Julius Seyler (Germany)	47·2	Peder Oestlund (Norway)	2:23·6
1899 Berlin	Peder Oestlund (Norway)	50·5	Peder Oestlund (Norway)	2:45·0
1900 Oslo	Peder Oestlund (Norway)	46·4	Edvard Engelsaas (Norway)	2:38·4
1901 Stockholm	Franz Wathèn (Finland)	54·0	Franz Wathèn (Finland)	2:43·4
1902 Helsinki	Rudolf Gundersen (Norway)	47·0	Rudolf Gundersen (Norway)	2:34·4
1903 Leningrad	Franz Wathèn (Finland)	49·4	Johan Schwartz (Norway)	2:59·0
1904 Oslo	Rudolf Gundersen (Norway)	46·6	Sigurd Mathisen (Norway)	2:35·8
1905 Groningen	Martinius Lördahl (Norway)	49·8	Coen de Koning (Netherlands)	2:41·0
1906 Helsinki	John Wikander (Finland)	50·8	Rudolf Gundersen (Norway)	2:41·6
1907 Trondheim	Oluf Steen (Norway)	47·4	Anti Wicklund (Finland)	2:33·0
1908 Davos	John Wikander (Finland)	44·8	Oscar Mathisen (Norway)	2:20·8
1909 Oslo	Oscar Mathisen (Norway)	45·6	Oscar Mathisen (Norway)	2:27·4
1910 Helsinki	Oscar Mathisen (Norway)	46·3	Oscar Mathisen (Norway)	2:32·6
1911 Trondheim	Nicolai Strunnikov (Russia)	46·4	Nicolai Strunnikov (Russia)	2:26·0

5000 metres	*Time*	*10000 metres*	*Time*	*Overall champion*
Jaap Eden (Netherlands)	9:59·0	Oscar Frederiksen (Norway)	20:21·4	Jaap Eden (Netherlands)
Einar Halvorsen (Norway)	9:32·0	Jaap Eden (Netherlands)	19:12·4	None declared
Jaap Eden (Netherlands)	8:41·0	Jaap Eden (Netherlands)	17:56·0	Jaap Eden (Netherlands)
Jaap Eden (Netherlands)	9:03·2	Jaap Eden (Netherlands)	18:52·4	Jaap Eden (Netherlands)
Jack McCulloch (Canada)	9:25·4	Jack McCulloch (Canada)	20:02·4	Jack McCulloch (Canada)
Peder Oestlund (Norway)	8:52·2	Peder Oestlund (Norway)	18:40·0	Peder Oestlund (Norway)
Peder Oestlund (Norway)	9:54·6	Jan Greve (Netherlands)	20:36·2	Peder Oestlund (Norway)
Edvard Engelsaas (Norway)	9:34·2	Edvard Engelsaas (Norway)	20:09·2	Edvard Engelsaas (Norway)
Rudolf Gundersen (Norway)	9:56·8	Franz Wathèn (Finland)	20:13·2	Franz Wathèn (Finland)
Jussi Wiinikainen (Finland)	9:20·6	Jussi Wiinikainen (Finland)	19:09·4	None declared
Gregory Kiselev (Russia)	10:08·0	Theodor Bönsnaes (Norway)	22:15·0	None declared
Sigurd Mathisen (Norway)	9:28·2	Sigurd Mathisen (Norway)	19:31·0	Sigurd Mathisen (Norway)
Coen de Koning (Netherlands)	9:17·6	Coen de Koning (Netherlands)	19:16·0	Coen de Koning (Netherlands)
Nicolai Sedov (Russia)	9:45·2	Nicolai Sedov (Russia)	19:03·6	None declared
Gunnar Strömsten (Finland)	9:27·6	Gunnar Strömsen (Finland)	19:09·4	None declared
Oscar Mathisen (Norway)	8:55·4	Oscar Mathisen (Norway)	18:01·8	Oscar Mathisen (Norway)
Evgeni Burnov (Russia)	8:45·0	Evgeni Burnov (Russia)	18:17·4	Oscar Mathisen (Norway)
Magnus Johansen (Norway)	9:27·9	Nicolai Strunnikov (Russia)	18:34·0	Nicolai Strunnikov (Russia)
Nicolai Strunnikov (Russia)	9:10·2	Nicolai Strunnikov (Russia)	18:13·0	Nicolai Strunnikov (Russia)

	500 metres	Time	1500 metres	Time
1912 Oslo	Oscar Mathisen (Norway)	44·2	Oscar Mathisen (Norway)	2:20·8
1913 Helsinki	Oscar Mathisen (Norway)	46·0	Oscar Mathisen (Norway)	2:24·4
1914 Oslo	Oscar Mathisen (Norway)	45·3	Oscar Mathisen (Norway)	2:26·1
1922 Oslo	Roald Larsen (Norway)	43·6	Clas Thunberg (Finland)	2:22·8
1923 Stockholm	Clas Thunberg (Finland)	45·2	Roald Larsen (Norway)	2:24·9
1924 Helsinki	Clas Thunberg (Finland)	45·0	Roald Larsen (Norway)	2:27·8
1925 Oslo	Clas Thunberg (Finland)	44·7	Clas Thunberg (Finland)	2:23·0
1926 Trondheim	Roald Larsen (Norway)	44·7	Ivar Ballangrud (Norway)	2:54·4
1927 Tampere	Clas Thunberg (Finland)	46·3	Clas Thunberg (Finland)	2:24·1
	Ismo Korpela (Finland)	46·3		
	Roald Larsen (Norway)	46·3		
1928 Davos	Roald Larsen (Norway)	43·1	Clas Thunberg (Finland)	2:18·8
1929 Oslo	Clas Thunberg (Finland)	43·1	Clas Thunberg (Finland)	2:21·9
1930 Oslo	Haakon Pedersen (Norway)	43·8	Michael Staksrud (Norway)	2:23·4
1931 Helsinki	Clas Thunberg (Finland)	44·4	Clas Thunberg (Finland)	2:24·4
1932 Lake Placid	Haakon Pedersen (Norway)	44·4	Ivar Ballangrud (Norway)	2:24·8
1933 Trondheim	Hans Engnestangen (Norway)	43·5	Clas Thunberg (Finland)	2:22·8
1934 Helsinki	Haakon Pedersen (Norway)	49·9	Bernt Evensen (Norway)	2:30·1
1935 Oslo	Harry Haraldsen (Norway)	43·6	Ivar Ballangrud (Norway)	2:23·4
1936 Davos	Delbert Lamb (USA)	42·6	Ivar Ballangrud (Norway)	2:17·4

5000 metres	*Time*	*10 000 metres*	*Time*	*Overall champion*
Oscar Mathisen (Norway)	8:45·2	Oscar Mathisen (Norway)	17:46·3	Oscar Mathisen (Norway)
Wasili Ippolitov (Russia)	8:43·4	Wasili Ippolitov (Russia)	17:37·8	Oscar Mathisen (Norway)
Oscar Mathisen (Norway)	9:20·6	Wasili Ippolitov (Russia)	18:47·6	Oscar Mathisen (Norway)
Harald Ström (Norway)	8:26·5	Harald Ström (Norway)	17:37·5	Harald Ström (Norway)
Jakob Melnikov (USSR)	9:06·2	Harald Ström (Norway)	17:58·4	Clas Thunberg (Finland)
Roald Larsen (Norway)	8:54·5	Uno Pietilä (Finland)	18:05·9	Roald Larsen (Norway)
Clas Thunberg (Finland)	8:43·3	Uno Pietilä (Finland)	18:01·5	Clas Thunberg (Finland)
Ivar Ballangrud (Norway)	8:42·7	Ivar Ballangrud (Norway)	18:09·1	Ivar Ballangrud (Norway)
Bernt Evensen (Norway)	8:53·5	Bernt Evensen (Norway)	18:05·8	Bernt Evensen (Norway)
Ivar Ballangrud (Norway)	8:28·8	Armand Carlsen (Norway)	17:17·4	Clas Thunberg (Finland)
Ivar Ballangrud (Norway)	9:03·2	Michael Staksrud (Norway)	17:57·0	Clas Thunberg (Finland)
Michael Staksrud (Norway)	8:28·7	Ivar Ballangrud (Norway)	17:53·7	Michael Staksrud (Norway)
Ossi Blomqvist (Finland)	8:58·6	Ossi Blomqvist (Finland)	18:22·2	Clas Thunberg (Finland)
Ivar Ballangrud (Norway)	8:37·6	Ivar Ballangrud (Norway)	17:58·0	Ivar Ballangrud (Norway)
Ivar Ballangrud (Norway)	8:42·5	Eddie Schroeder (USA)	17:43·6	Hans Engnestangen (Norway)
Birger Wasenius (Finland)	10:03·0	Armand Carlsen (Norway)	19:03·5	Bernt Evensen (Norway)
Michael Staksrud (Norway)	8:30·0	Michael Staksrud (Norway)	17:48·5	Michael Staksrud (Norway)
Ivar Ballangrud (Norway)	8:32·5	Birger Wasenius (Finland)	17:51·4	Ivar Ballangrud (Norway)

I

	500 metres	*Time*	*1500 metres*	*Time*
1937 Oslo	Georg Grog (Norway)	42·9	Hans Engenstangen (Norway)	2:19·5
1938 Davos	Hans Engenstangen (Norway)	41·8	Hans Engnestangen (Norway)	2:15·9
1939 Helsinki	Hans Engenstangen (Norway)	44·8	Birger Wasenius (Finland)	2:30·7
1947 Oslo	Sverre Farstad (Norway)	44·3	Sverre Farstad (Norway)	2:21·0
1948 Helsinki	Konst. Kudrjavtsev (USSR)	43·9	John Werket (USA)	2:22·3
1949 Oslo	Ken Henry (USA)	46·3	John Werket (USA)	2:30·8
1950 Eskilstuna	John Werket (USA)	47·3	John Werket (USA)	2:32·1
1951 Davos	Susomo Naito (Japan)	43·0	Wim van der Voort (Netherlands)	2:17·7
1952 Hamar	Ken Henry (USA)	43·4	Wim van der Voort (Netherlands)	2:21·3
1953 Helsinki	Toivo Salonen (Finland)	43·1	Boris Schilkov (USSR)	2:18·1
1954 Sapporo	Eugeni Grishin (USSR)	44·1	Boris Schilkov (USSR)	2:22·3
1955 Moscow	Toivo Salonen (Finland)	42·6	Oleg Goncharenko (USSR)	2:20·6
1956 Oslo	Juri Michailov (USSR)	41·9	Boris Schilkov (USSR)	2:11·6
1957 Ostersund	Eugeni Grishin (USSR)	42·3	Boris Schilkov (USSR)	2:13·9
1958 Helsinki	Robert Merkulov (USSR)	44·2	Oleg Goncharenko (USSR)	2:17·7
1959 Oslo	Genadi Voronin (USSR)	42·4	Toivo Salonen (Finland)	2:15·8
1960 Davos	Eugeni Grishin (USSR)	40·5	Boris Stenin (USSR)	2:10·7
1961 Gothenburg	Eugeni Grishin (USSR)	41·7	Henk van der Grift (Netherlands)	2:17·8
1962 Moscow	Eugeni Grishin (USSR)	41·7	Boris Stenin (USSR)	2:13·5
1963 Karuizawa	Eugeni Grishin (USSR)	39·8	Lu Chih-huan (China)	2:09·2

5000 metres	Time	10 000 metres	Time	Overall champion
Max Stiepl (Austria)	8:28·6	Max Stiepl (Austria)	17:25·3	Michael Staksrud (Norway)
Ivar Ballangrud (Norway)	8:20·2	Ivar Ballangrud (Norway)	17:14·4	Ivar Ballangrud (Norway)
Charles Matthiesen (Norway)	9:31·0	Alfons Berzins (USSR)	19:19·5	Birger Wasenius (Finland)
Lassi Parkkinen (Finland)	8:33·7	Reidar Liaklev (Norway)	17:37·0	Lassi Parkkinen (Finland)
Kees Broekman (Netherlands)	8:37·5	Kees Broekman (Netherlands)	17:48·8	Odd Lundberg (Norway)
Kornél Pajor (Hungary)	9:09·4	Kornél Pajor (Hungary)	18:42·0	Kornél Pajor (Hungary)
Hjalmar Andersen (Norway)	9:15·4	Hjalmar Andersen (Norway)	17:40·8	Hjalmar Andersen (Norway)
Hjalmar Andersen (Norway)	8:27·9	Hjalmar Andersen (Norway)	19:31·8	Hjalmar Andersen (Norway)
Hjalmar Andersen (Norway)	8:16·8	Hjalmar Andersen (Norway)	17:03·5	Hjalmar Andersen (Norway)
Oleg Goncharenko (USSR)	8:26·0	Oleg Goncharenko (USSR)	17:22·2	Oleg Goncharenko (USSR)
Oleg Goncharenko (USSR)	8:21·9	Oleg Goncharenko (USSR)	17:38·7	Boris Schilkov (USSR)
Knut Johannesen (Norway)	8:33·0	Sigge Ericsson (Sweden)	17:09·8	Sigge Ericsson (Sweden)
Oleg Goncharenko (USSR)	8:07·7	Torstein Selersten (Norway)	16:43·3	Oleg Goncharenko (USSR)
Knut Johannesen (Norway)	8:08·9	Knut Johannesen (Norway)	16:33·9	Knut Johannesen (Norway)
Vlad. Schilikovski (USSR)	8:31·5	Knut Johannesen (Norway)	17:08·3	Oleg Goncharenko (USSR)
Jan Pesman (Netherlands)	8:12·1	Knut Johannesen (Norway)	17:00·8	Juhani Järvinen (Finland)
Valeri Kotov (USSR)	8:06·1	Jan Pesman (Netherlands)	16:53·7	Boris Stenin (USSR)
Ivar Nilsson (Sweden)	7:58·0	Viktor Kosichkin (USSR)	16:35·9	Henk van der Grift (Netherlands)
Ivar Nilsson (Sweden)	8:03·2	Jonny Nilsson (Sweden)	16:29·4	Viktor Kosichkin (USSR)
Jonny Nilsson (Sweden)	7:34·3	Jonny Nilsson (Sweden)	15:33·0	Jonny Nilsson (Sweden)

	500 metres	Time	1500 metres	Time
1964 Helsinki	Keiichi Suzuki (Japan)	41·1	Nils Aaness (Norway)	2:12·0
1965 Oslo	Keiichi Suzuki (Japan)	40·7	Per Ivar Moe (Norway)	2:08·0
1966 Gothenburg	Tom Gray (USA)	40·9	Kees Verkerk (Netherlands)	2:12·9
1967 Oslo	Keiichi Suzuki (Japan)	40·9	Ard Schenk (Netherlands)	2:08·1
1968 Gothenburg	Keiichi Suzuki (Japan)	40·3	Magne Thomassen (Norway)	2:07·1
1969 Deventer	Keiichi Suzuki (Japan)	40·1	Kees Verkerk (Netherlands)	2:08·7
1970 Oslo	Magne Thomassen (Norway)	40·15	Ard Schenk (Netherlands)	2:04·4
1971 Gothenburg	Dag Fornaess (Norway)	40·31	Ard Schenk (Netherlands)	2:04·8
1972 Oslo	Ard Schenk (Netherlands)	40·14	Ard Schenk (Netherlands)	2:03·06
	Roar Grönvold (Norway)	40·14		
1973 Deventer	Bill Lanigan (USA)	42·00	Sten Stensen (Norway)	2:12·70
1974 Inzell	Masaki Suzuki (Japan)	40·0	Hans van Helden (Netherlands)	2:01·90

Women's World Ice Speed Skating Champions

	500 metres	Time	1000 metres	Time
1936 Stockholm	Kit Klein (USA)	53·3	Verné Lesche (Finland)	1:53·6
1937 Davos	Laila Nilsen (Norway)	46·4	Laila Nilsen (Norway)	1:38·8
1938 Oslo	Laila Nilsen (Norway)	50·7	Laila Nilsen (Norway)	1:40·3
1939 Tampere	Glou Donker (Netherlands)	54·3	Verné Lesche (Finland)	1:55·9
1947 Drammen	Verné Lesche (Finland)	52·7	Verné Lesche (Finland)	1:53·9
1948 Turku	Lidia Selikhova (USSR)	49·7	Maria Isakova (USSR)	1:42·8

5000 metres	Time	10 000 metres	Time	Overall champion
Knut Johannesen (Norway)	7:41·3	Knut Johannesen (Norway)	16:08·9	Knut Johannesen (Norway)
Jonny Nilsson (Sweden)	7:33·2	Jonny Nilsson (Sweden)	15:47·7	Per Ivar Moe (Norway)
Kees Verkerk (Netherlands)	7:42·8	Kees Verkerk (Netherlands)	16:21·6	Kees Verkerk (Netherlands)
Kees Verkerk (Netherlands)	7:30·4	Kees Verkerk (Netherlands)	15:51·7	Kees Verkerk (Netherlands)
Anton Maier (Norway)	7:25·0	Anton Maier (Norway)	15:26·8	Anton Maier (Norway)
Kees Verkerk (Netherlands)	7:24·1	Jan Bols (Netherlands)	16:02·9	Dag Fornaess (Norway)
Jan Bols (Netherlands)	7:28·6	Jan Bols (Netherlands)	15:22·6	Ard Schenk (Netherlands)
Ard Schenk (Netherlands)	7:18·8	Ard Schenk (Netherlands)	15:0·16	Ard Schenk (Netherlands)
Ard Schenk (Netherlands)	7:22·84	Ard Schenk (Netherlands)	15:22·09	Ard Schenk (Netherlands)
Göran Claeson (Sweden)	7:47·03	Göran Claeson (Sweden)	15:45·98	Göran Claeson (Sweden)
Sten Stensen (Norway)	7:23·55	Sten Stensen (Norway)	15:18·55	Sten Stensen (Norway)

3000 metres	Time	5000 metres	Time	Overall champion
Kit Klein (USA)	6:12·0	Verné Lesche (Finland)	10:15·3	Kit Klein (USA)
Laila Nilsen (Norway)	5:29·6	Laila Nilsen (Norway)	9:28·3	Laila Nilsen (Norway)
Verné Lesche (Finland)	5:53·0	Verné Lesche (Finland)	9:43·6	Laila Nilsen (Norway)
Verné Lesche (Finland)	6:2·03	Verné Lesche (Finland)	10:27·6	Verné Lesche (Finland)
Verné Lesche (Finland)	5:43·8	Verné Lesch (Finland)	9:51·7	Verné Lesche (Finland)
Maria Isakova (USSR)	5:34·9	Verné Lesche (Finland)	9:39·5	Maria Isakova (USSR)

	500 metres	Time	1000 metres	Time
1949 Kongsberg	Maria Isakova (USSR)	48·2	Maria Isakova (USSR)	1:41·9
	Mariana Valovova (USSR)	48·2	Zoia Kholtschevnikova (USSR)	1:41·9
1950 Moscow	Maria Isakova (USSR)	49·9	Tatjana Karelina (USSR)	1:49·2
1951 Eskilstuna	Randi Thorwaldsen (Norway)	49·4	Eevi Huttunen (Finland)	1:42·5
1952 Gamlakarleby	Natalia Dontshenko (USSR)	50·4	Lidia Selikhova (USSR)	1:43·0
1953 Lillehammer	Rimma Zhukova (USSR)	48·3	Rimma Zhukova (USSR)	1:38·5
1954 Ostersund	Sofia Kondakova (USSR)	47·6	Sofia Kondakova (USSR)	1:40·2
1955 Kuopio	Tamara Rylova (USSR)	48·9	Sofia Kondakova (USSR)	1:40·9
1956 Kvarnsveden	Sofia Kondakova (USSR)	47·9	Sofia Kondakova (USSR)	1:40·2
1957 Imatra	Sofia Kondakova (USSR)	48·8	Inga Artamonova (USSR)	1:39·9
1958 Kristinehamn	Tamara Rylova (USSR)	47·6	Sofia Kondakova (USSR)	1:43·3
1959 Sverdlovsk	Tamara Rylova (USSR)	47·5	Tamara Rylova (USSR)	1:41·0
	Sofia Kondakova (USSR)	47·5		
1960 Ostersund	Lidia Skoblikova (USSR)	49·5	Klara Guseva (USSR)	1:40·2
1961 Tönsberg	Valentina Stenina (USSR)	48·1	Valentina Stenina (USSR)	1:37·8
1962 Imatra	Elvira Seroczynska (Poland)	47·6	Inga Artamonova (USSR)	1:41·6
1963 Karuizawa	Lidia Sloblikova (USSR)	45·4	Lidia Skoblikova (USSR)	1:31·8
1964 Kristinehamn	Irina Egorova (USSR)	46·2	Lidia Skoblikova (USSR)	1:34·9
	Lidia Skoblikova (USSR)	46·2		

3000 metres	Time	5000 metres	Time	Overall champion
Maria Isakova (USSR)	5:29·7	Verné Lesche (Finland)	9:26·8	Maria Isakova (USSR)
Rimma Zhukova (USSR)	5:36·8	Zinaida Krotova (USSR)	11:12·9	Maria Isakova (USSR)
Eevi Huttunen (Finland)	5:39·1	Eevi Huttunen (Finland)	9:45·8	Eevi Huttunen (Finland)
Maria Anikanova (USSR)	5:41·5	Rimma Zhukova (USSR)	9:32·4	Lidia Selikhova (USSR)
Khalida Schegoleeva (USSR)	5:25·8	Eevi Huttunen (Finland)	9:06·1	Khalida Schegoleeva (USSR)
Rimma Zhukova (USSR)	5:26·3	Eevi Huttunen (Finland)	9:20·2	Lidia Selikhova (USSR)
Rimma Zhukova (USSR)	5:33·1	Rimma Zhukova (USSR)	9:26·4	Rimma Zhukova (USSR)

		1500 metres	Time	
Rimma Zhukova (USSR)	5:32·7	Sofia Kondakova (USSR)	2:38·0	Sofia Kondakova (USSR)
Eevi Huttunen (Finland)	5:33·8	Inga Artamonova (USSR)	2:37·0	Inga Artamonova (USSR)
Inga Artamonova (USSR)	5:33·0	Inga Artamonova (USSR)	2:34·3	Inga Artamonova (USSR)
Eevi Huttunen (Finland)	5:30·3	Inga Artamonova (USSR)	2:31·6	Tamara Rylova (USSR)
Lidia Skoblikova (USSR)	5:23·9	Valentina Stenina (USSR)	2:37·6	Valentina Stenina (USSR)
Inga Artamonova (USSR)	5:23·4	Valentina Stenina (USSR)	2:33·3	Valentina Stenina (USSR)
Inga Artamonova (USSR)	5:27·3	Inga Artamonova (USSR)	2:32·2	Inga Artamonova (USSR)
Lidia Skoblikova (USSR)	5:10·5	Lidia Skoblikova (USSR)	2:23·3	Lidia Skoblikova (USSR)
Lidia Skoblikova (USSR)	5:11·4	Lidia Skoblikova (USSR)	2:26·7	Lidia Skoblikova (USSR)

	500 metres	*Time*	*1000 metres*	*Time*
1965 Oulu	Inga Artamonova (USSR)	46·8	Inga Artamonova (USSR)	1:37·7
1966 Trondheim	Irina Egorova (USSR)	46·9	Tatjana Rastopsjina (USSR)	1:35·9
1967 Deventer	Mary Meyers (USA)	46·0	Stien Kaiser (Netherlands)	1:36·2
1968 Helsinki	Ludmila Titova (USSR)	46·2	Ludmila Titova (USSR)	1:34·5
1969 Grenoble	Kirsti Biermann (Norway)	45·1	Lasma Kauniste (USSR)	1:31·2
1970 West Allis	Ludmila Titova (USSR)	45·38	Ludmila Titova (USSR)	1:32·6
			Sigrid Sundby (Norway)	1:32·6
1971 Helsinki	Anne Henning (USA)	44·6	Dianne Holum (USA)	1:33·0
1972 Heerenveen	Sheila Young (USA)	44·20	Dianne Holum (USA)	1:31·88
1973 Strömsund	Sheila Young (USA)	43·56	Atje Keulen-Deelstra (Netherlands)	1:30·41
1974 Heerenveen	Sheila Young (USA)	44·44	Atje Keulen-Deelstra (Netherlands)	1:28·91

3000 metres	Time	1500 metres	Time	Overall champion
Inga Artamonova (USSR)	5:18·2	Valentina Stenina (USSR)	2:27·5	Inga Artamonova (USSR)
Stien Kaiser (Netherlands)	5:06·6	Song Soon Kim (North Korea)	2:29·4	Valentina Stenina (USSR)
Stien Kaiser (Netherlands)	5:18·7	Stien Kaiser (Netherlands)	2:23·0	Stien Kaiser (Netherlands)
Ans Schut (Netherlands)	5:04·8	Stien Kaiser (Netherlands)	2:26·4	Stien Kaiser (Netherlands)
Ans Schut (Netherlands)	4:52·0	Stien Kaiser (Netherlands)	2:21·5	Lasma Kauniste (USSR)
Ans Schut (Netherlands)	4·56·2	Ans Schut (Netherlands)	2:23·3	Atje Keulen-Deelstra (Netherlands)
Stien Kaiser (Netherlands)	4:57·5	Nina Statkevich (USSR)	2:23·2	Nina Statkevich (USSR)
Stien Kaiser (Netherlands)	4:54·62	Atje Keulen-Deelstra (Netherlands)	2:17·98	Atje Keulen-Deelstra (Netherlands)
Sippie Tichelaar (Netherlands)	4:50·26	Galina Stapanskaya (USSR)	2:20·88	Atje Keulen-Deelstra (Netherlands)
Atje Keulen-Deelstra (Netherlands)	4:49·07	Atje Keulen-Deelstra (Netherlands)	2:19·07	Atje Keulen-Deelstra (Netherlands)

(From 1956, the women's 1500 metres replaced the 5000.)

World Ice Hockey Championships

		Gold	Silver	Bronze
1920	Antwerp	Canada	USA	Czechoslovakia
1924	Chamonix	Canada	USA	Great Britain
1928	St Moritz	Canada	Sweden	Switzerland
1930	Chamonix	Canada	Germany	Switzerland
1931	Krynica	Canada	USA	Austria
1932	Lake Placid	Canada	USA	Germany
1933	Prague	USA	Canada	Czechoslovakia
1934	Milan	Canada	USA	Germany
1935	Davos	Canada	Switzerland	Great Britain
1936	Garmisch	Great Britain	Canada	USA
1937	London	Canada	Great Britain	Switzerland
1938	Prague	Canada	Great Britain	Czechoslovakia
1939	Zürich	Canada	USA	Switzerland
1947	Prague	Czechoslovakia	Sweden	Austria
1948	St Moritz	Canada	Czechoslovakia	Switzerland
1949	Stockholm	Czechoslovakia	Canada	USA
1950	London	Canada	USA	Switzerland
1951	Paris	Canada	Sweden	Switzerland
1952	Oslo	Canada	USA	Sweden
1953	Zürich	Sweden	West Germany	Switzerland
1954	Stockholm	USSR	Canada	Sweden
1955	Düsseldorf	Canada	USSR	Czechoslovakia
1956	Cortina	USSR	USA	Canada
1957	Moscow	Sweden	USSR	Czechoslovakia
1958	Oslo	Canada	USSR	Sweden
1959	Prague	Canada	USSR	Czechoslovakia
1960	Squaw Valley	USA	Canada	USSR
1961	Geneva	Canada	Czechoslovakia	USSR
1962	Colorado Springs	Sweden	Canada	USA
1963	Stockholm	USSR	Sweden	Czechoslovakia
1964	Innsbruck	USSR	Sweden	Czechoslovakia
1965	Tampere	USSR	Czechoslovakia	Sweden
1966	Ljubljana	USSR	Czechoslovakia	Canada
1967	Vienna	USSR	Sweden	Canada
1968	Grenoble	USSR	Czechoslovakia	Canada
1969	Stockholm	USSR	Sweden	Czechoslovakia
1970	Stockholm	USSR	Sweden	Czechoslovakia
1971	Geneva	USSR	Czechoslovakia	Sweden
1972	Prague	Czechoslovakia	USSR	Sweden
1973	Moscow	USSR	Sweden	Czechoslovakia
1974	Helsinki	USSR	Czechoslovakia	Sweden

22. *Olympic Review*

Although the ISU has always regarded its annual world champion-ships, in both figure and speed skating, as of prior importance to the Olympic competitions, there is little doubt that most skaters cherish an Olympic gold medal above a world title. This surely has a lot to do with the far greater publicity which the Olympic events enjoy, graced as they now are by the presence of more news reporters than competitors, and watched on the home screens by countless millions of televiewers.

London, 1908

Figure skating was included in the Olympic schedule before other ice and snow sports, sixteen years before the first separate Winter Olympics were held. The ready accessibility of the Prince's Skating Club indoor ice rink allowed the sport's convenient inclusion in the fourth Summer Olympic Games, in London in 1908. The twenty skaters who took part represented six nations – Argentine, Germany, Great Britain, Russia, Sweden and the United States.

Ulrich Salchow of Sweden took the men's title by a 3–2 judges' decision over his compatriot, Richard Johansson. Third-placed Per Thorén gave Sweden a grand slam. Britain's Madge Syers gained a comfortable women's victory over Elsa Rendschmidt, the German runner-up. In those days Mrs Syers compared favourably with most men and in fact competed with them in

early world championships, finishing second to Salchow in
1902.

The pairs title went to the Germans, Heinrich Burger and
Anna Hübler, with Britain's James and Phyllis Johnson runners-
up. In third place, Edgar and Madge Syers were probably handi-
capped by the training needs of two events.

Antwerp, 1920

Because of the First World War, the second Olympic contest in
figure skating was not held until 1920, when ice hockey was
added to the programme at Antwerp Ice Palace, boosting the
total ice events entries to seventy-three men and twelve women
from ten nations.

Sweden's Gillis Grafström, originator of the flying sit-spin,
succeeded his compatriot, Salchow, as men's figure skating champion. Salchow, still competing at 42, was fourth of nine competitors despite a knee injury. Magda Julin-Mauroy, another
Swede, narrowly won the women's title from her fellow country-
woman, Svea Norén, but the competition's highest scoring free-
skater was the third-placed American, Theresa Weld, later to
become editor of the US magazine, *Skating*. Walter and Ludowika
Jakobsson stylishly gained the pairs title for Finland.

The ice hockey début did much to advance the sport's European
popularity. Seven teams competed and it mattered little that the
Canadian victors and American runners-up were in a class apart
from Europe's best. The Czechs and Swedes in turn stood out
from the rest. Switzerland was humiliated 29–0 by the United
States, who lost 2–0 in their key match with Canada.

Chamonix, 1924

In the first self-contained, separate Winter Olympic Games,
thirty-one speed skaters, twenty-nine figure skaters and eighty-
two ice hockey players swelled the number of competitors on
skates to 142. The figure skaters included the only women partici-

pating, thirteen in all, of whom five took part in the pairs event as well as performing as soloists. Three of the men soloists also entered the pairs, making a total of eight figure skaters in dual roles, nowadays generally considered too difficult to attempt because the simultaneous training requirements would mean leaving one's partner too often on the sidelines.

The ice stadium, admirable by the standards of the time, was a complex arena including a 400-metre speed skating perimeter around two ice hockey rinks, with the end semicircles used by figure skaters.

Clas Thunberg, the Finnish speed skater, won three gold medals, a silver and a bronze. One of his gold medals was, in a sense, complimentary, because it was also awarded for being the best overall performer in the four distances, the only time a combination award has been made for Olympic speed skating. He convincingly won the two middle distances, 1500 and 5000 metres, finished second to his fellow Finn, Julius Skutnabb, in the 10000 metres, and tied for third place in the 500-metre sprint won by the American, Charles Jewtraw.

The individual gold figure skating medals each went to respected 'greats' in the sport's history. Gillis Grafström, of Sweden, placed first by only four of the seven judges, gained a narrow verdict over his Austrian rival, Willy Böckl.

Herma Plank-Szabó, one of the early Viennese stalwarts and world champion for five consecutive years from 19??, took the women's title by unanimous vote. Beatrix Loughran, the American runner-up, was followed by Britain's Ethel Muckelt, with an endearingly diminutive Sonja Henie last in a field of eight at the age of 11. But, even then, the connoisseur could detect unquestionable potential in the Norwegian's smoothly landed jumps and graceful spins. She was afterwards to reign as queen of the ice with three Olympic and ten world championship crowns.

In the pairs contest, Alfred Berger and Helene Engelmann struck another blow for the Viennese school of technique by outpointing the then better known Finns, Walter and Ludowika Jakobsson. The composition of the partnerships following them underlined the frequency in those days of doubling in solo and pairs events. Andrée Joly, third with Pierre Brunet, was also fifth among the women. The British pair who finished fourth were John Page, the fifth-placed man, and Miss Muckelt, the women's bronze medallist.

The ice hockey tournament was, as always since, the big spectator draw and Europeans were again dazzled by a transatlantic level which the Continental teams were unable to match. Goals galore in uneven games seldom failed to mesmerize onlookers, who admired and respected a brand of play to which they had not been accustomed.

Canada overwhelmed the rest and the United States team, even though overshadowed by the Canadians, also outclassed the best Europe could offer. The eight contenders were divided into two groups, the top two in each qualifying for a final pool of four. These were, Canada, USA, Great Britain and Sweden, finishing in that order.

Canada scored 33 goals without reply against Switzerland. This, not surprisingly, still stands as the Olympic scoring record – an astonishing average rate of less than 2 minutes per goal throughout 60 minutes' play. The Canadians also defeated Czechoslovakia 30–0 and Sweden 22–0. Their least one-sided game was a 6–1 victory over USA – the Americans' only defeat. Great Britain, though losing 2–19, was the only side to score more than once against the champions. A 4–3 win against Sweden, the only match decided by the odd goal, earned Britain the bronze medal.

St Moritz, 1928

The Finnish speed skater, Clas Thunberg, although approaching 35, proved still a master in 1928 by winning two gold medals for the two shorter distances. But in the 500-metre sprint, Norwegian Bernt Evensen also took a gold with an equal time, the first Winter Olympic occasion when two golds were awarded for an individuals' event. The 5000 metres revealed the early world-beating class of another Norwegian, Ivar Ballangrud, later to be recognized as an all-time great.

The figure skating saw the last of Gillis Grafström's three men's victories for Sweden and the first of Sonja Henie's three women's wins for Norway – a master at his peak and a prodigy on the way up. The Austrian, Willy Böckl, closely challenged Grafström all the way, while Miss Henie enjoyed a more comfortable passage and introduced a refreshingly more athletic element in women's freestyle. In the pairs event, Pierre Brunet and Andrée Joly set a high standard in well timed lifts.

The ice hockey tournament emphasized the still wide gulf between the Canadians and the ten other competing nations. The USA did not enter and the Canadians, because of their palpable superiority, were granted exemption until the semi-finals, to be joined by Sweden, Switzerland and Great Britain. Scoring double figures without conceding a goal against each of the other three (an aggregate of 38–0), Canada displayed complete mastery while the Swedes proved best of the rest by defeating Switzerland 4–0 and Great Britain 3–1. The Swiss beat the British to take the bronze medal.

Lake Placid, 1932

Sonja Henie, at the zenith of her form, won the second of her three Olympic figure skating victories at the third Winter Olympic Games, with a unanimous judges' verdict over Fritzi Burger, the Austrian runner-up. But even Sonja's magnetism was over-shadowed by the fascinated interest in the men's event. Could that remarkable Swede, Gillis Grafström, win for a fourth successive time at the incredible age of 38?

The new man of the moment was Austrian Karl Schäfer, at 22 a babe by comparison. Schäfer won a thrilling tussle by a 5–2 decision and went on to succeed again four years later. In fairness to Grafström, it must be recorded that a knee injury hampered his performance and probably cost him the distinction of becoming the only person to win an Olympic event for a fourth time. As it was, he still finished clearly ahead of the third-placed Canadian, Montgomery Wilson.

The pairs title was retained by the French couple, Pierre and Andrée Brunet, who had married since their previous victory. Their nearest challengers, Americans Sherwin Badger and Beatrix

Loughran, came close enough to take better marks from two of the seven judges.

American successes over all four speed skating distances – two each by Jack Shea and Irving Jaffee – were gained with more than ordinary home ice advantages. For the only time in any Olympic or world speed skating championship, the customary international rules of racing in pairs were temporarily suspended in deference to the American-style 'pack' starts with heats and finals.

This meant a revolution in tactics so far as the European competitors were concerned, the strategy of spurting and the use of elbowing technique being completely new to them. The redoubtable Finn, Clas Thunberg, declined to compete in these controversial circumstances and the only two Europeans able to gain medals were the Norwegians, Ivar Ballangrud – the outstanding racer of that era – and Bernt Evensen, second in the 10 000 metres and 500 metres respectively.

Shea equalled the Olympic record for the 500 metres with a time of 43·4 seconds. But his victory in the 1500 metres and both the Jaffee longer distance wins were the slowest Olympic successes ever recorded. The Americans were significantly outpaced during the annual world championships, held later on the same track under the normal two-at-a-time racing rules, when Ballangrud won every event.

The ice hockey tournament, a third success in this event for Canada, was notable for a closer American challenge than before and for the smallest entry the Olympic series has ever had. With Germany and Poland Europe's sole representatives, only four teams competed – each playing the other twice. In the two Canada-USA matches which settled the issue, the Canadians won the first 2–1 in extra time and drew the other 2–2 after three additional periods.

Garmisch, 1936

A disbelieving 14 000 packed the elaborate new Olympic Ice Stadium to watch Carl Erhardt lead Britain's ice hockey players in an historic defeat of Canada, the acknowledged masters of the game who had won every previous Olympic contest. This dramatic form upset was brought about by beating the Canadians 2–1 and, in the final game, holding the United States to a scoreless draw sufficient for overall victory.

In those pre-television days Bob Giddens, then a distinguished writer on the sport, recorded how Britain received the news from the BBC radio commentator, Bob Bowman: 'Almost hysterical but brilliantly fluent, Bowman poured excited words into his mike which told folks with their heads halfway down their loudspeakers that now, before his eyes, the British team had achieved a miracle. By beating Canada, Britain had cured the complex, so deeply bedded in European minds, that Canada was invincible.'

The figure skating inevitably will be remembered most for the third Olympic victory of Sonja Henie, who became a legend in her own time. But whereas the great Sonja had clearly dominated four years previously, the gap between her rivals had now decreased. Though eight years Sonja's junior, Britain's Cecilia Colledge, who was to become world champion the following season, proved a dangerous challenger. No longer did Sonja enjoy a unanimous verdict, one judge placing the two girls equal, and the Norwegian was probably wise to turn professional soon afterwards.

Karl Schäfer, a star pupil of the Vienna Skating School's most glorious era, comfortably retained the men's crown he had captured in 1932. His nearest challenger, Ernst Baier, was compensated with a hard-earned victory for Germany in the pairs contest, partnered by his future wife, Maxi Herber. It was something of a cliff-hanger, with a young Viennese brother and sister, Erich and Ilse Pausin, stealing the spectators' hearts with a skilful interpretation of a lilting Strauss waltz. The Germans' more experienced technique split the judges 7–2 in their favour.

But the real star of the Garmisch Games was Norwegian speed skater Ivar Ballangrud. In his third Olympics and less than a month from his thirty-second birthday, Ballangrud won three gold medals, for the 500, 5000 and 10000 metres, and alos took

K

the silver in the 1500 metres, just one second slower than his fellow countryman, Charles Mathiesen.

St Moritz, 1948

The fifth Winter Olympic meeting was originally scheduled for 1940 at Sapporo, Japan, but the Second World War intervened and Sapporo had to wait another thirty-two years. The selection of St Moritz for a second time was influenced by early post-war conditions when the Games were resumed in 1948.

The figure skating saw a transatlantic freestyle eclipse by American Dick Button and Canadian Barbara Ann Scott. They gave Europe a first glimpse of the new American school of theatrical athleticism in jumps. Displaying physical strength and suppleness, Button was the forerunner of a revolutionary trend that was to characterize future men's free-skating.

The more orthodox Swiss, Hans Gerschwiler, held second place only by virtue of his figures, outpointed in free-skating by another American, John Lettengarver. Miss Scott serenely withstood fierce pressure from Britain's Jeannette Altwegg in the women's figures and by the Austrian, Eva Pawlik, in the free-skating. The Belgians, Pierre Baugniet and Micheline Lannoy, a gracefully authentic partnership, clinched the pairs title after a resolute Hungarian bid from Ede Király and Andrea Kékesy.

Norwegians won three of the four speed skating events. Finn Helgesen snatched the 500 metres by a tenth of a second from his compatriot, Thomas Bryberg, and the two Americans, Ken Bartholomew and Robert Fitzgerald, whose equal times earned the first Winter Olympic triple tie for silver medals.

Sverre Farstad won the 1500 metres and Reidar Liaklev the 5000. But the Swede, Åke Seyffarth, was the most noteworthy speed skater on view. Decisive winner of the 10000 metres with nearly ten seconds to spare, he was also runner-up in the 1500 – a powerful racer who had passed his peak form, having established world records over two distances during the war years.

The Canadians recaptured the ice hockey title, avenging their unexpected defeat by the British in 1936, but only by a goal-average verdict over the Czechs. Each won seven of their eight matches, their direct encounter ending in a rare goal-less stalemate. The Czech line-up included a player who gained greater fame as a tennis player, Jaroslav Drobny.

Oslo, 1952

The outstanding individual of these Games was the Norwegian speed skater, Hjalmar Andersen, who took three gold medals for the 1500, 5000 and 10000 metres, setting new Olympic times for the two longest distances. His strength at the time is underlined by the fact that, only a week previously at Hamar, Norway, he set a world record for 10000 metres which stood until 1960. Ken Henry won the 500 metres sprint for the United States.

Dick Button repeated his 1948 success in the men's figure skating, when the stress and strain of arduous practice led to his achieving the first real triple loop jump in a comfortable victory. Excellent figure tracings gained the women's gold medal for Britain's Jeannette Altwegg, even though she was surpassed in free-skating by the spectacular French girl, Jacqueline du Bief, and two Americans, Tenley Albright and Virginia Baxter.

This was Miss Altwegg's farewell championship appearance and instead of following the vogue to capitalize in professional ranks, she won worldwide admiration by accepting a post at the Pestalozzi children's village at Trogen, Switzerland. The pair skating went to the German husband and wife team, Paul and Ria Falk, whose precision timing in lifts and skilful 'shadow' jumps and spins was superb.

Nine nations contested the ice hockey tournament, again won by the Canadians, but this sixth success in seven Olympics was to prove their last for a very long time. In eight games Canada conceded only one point, in a tie with the USA. The Americans were runners up after losing one match to the Swedes, who finished level third on points with the Czechs. In an exciting bronze-medal decider, Sweden won 5–3 after the Czechs had established a three-goal lead.

Cortina, 1956

An unprecedented spate of speed skating records on the Lake Misurina circuit was due to rapidly improving techniques at high altitude. In the four events, three skaters set new world records. A total of seventy-three competitors were inside the previous best Olympic times for their distances and forty-one new national records were established.

In their first Olympics, Soviet racers got four gold medals for winning three events because compatriots Juri Michailov and Eugeni Grishin tied in the 1500 metres, each clocking a new world-record time. Grishin, the outstanding ice sprinter of his day, also established a fresh world time to win the 500 metres. For the first time since 1932, Norway failed to get a speed skating first.

The technical and spectacular highlight of the figure skating was the free-skating of the men's dominant American trio, Hayes Jenkins, Ronnie Robertson and David Jenkins, who finished in that order. Hayes Jenkins won by virtue of a slender lead in the figures, and although his free-skating was excellent, the contents of his programme were not quite so ambitious as those displayed by Robertson, who was a sensational, at times almost acrobatic, free-skater. He gave everything he had on this occasion. He touched a hand down when landing a triple loop jump, then completed a triple salchow to perfection and concluded with a fast cross-toe spin, altogether a thrilling programme for the mesmerized audience.

In the women's contest Tenley Albright, runner-up in the previous Winter Olympics to Britain's Jeannette Altwegg, presented a wonderfully delicate programme, dramatically timed to *The Tales of Hoffmann* in a seemingly effortless, graceful style, ending worthily with a rapid cross-foot spin. But if a miracle was needed by Carol Heiss to overtake her brilliant compatriot, this she so nearly achieved. Very speedy and impressive, she not only scored almost as many marks as Tenley, but was actually placed first in the free-skating by five of the eleven judges (nowadays nine judges are considered enough).

The elegant Viennese partnership, Kurt Oppelt and Sissy

Schwarz, gained a controversial verdict over Canada's Norris Bowden and Frances Dafoe in the pairs event, both couples synchronizing superbly.

At their first Olympic ice hockey attempt, the Russians emerged victorious and unbeaten in their five final pool matches against the United States runners-up, third-placed Canada, Sweden, Czechoslovakia and Germany. Scoring 25 goals and conceding only 5, the Soviet players never looked unduly ruffled. Their clever stick-handling and superior skating, both in defence and attack, decided the issue in the two games that mattered most, defeating USA 4–0 and Canada 2–0.

Squaw Valley, 1960

Five inside the world record, eight inside the Olympic record and twelve inside their national records – *all* in one event. That, in the history-making 10 000 metres, was the speed skating highlight of the second Winter Olympics to be held outside Europe. Norwegian Knut Johannesen fairly whistled through to chop 46 seconds off the 1952 record established by the great Hjalmar Andersen. Even Britain's Terence Monaghan, who came fifth, was a full second faster than Andersen's previous world's best.

Eugeni Grishin equalled his own world record time of 40·2 seconds in winning the 500 metres for USSR, emphasizing that, at 28, he still had no peers as a sprinter. He also tied with the Norwegian, Roald Aas, to share the 1500-metre gold medal award. In the 5000 metres, Russian Viktor Kosichkin was nearly 10 seconds faster than Johannesen.

Women's speed skating was included in the Olympics for the first time and another Russian, Lidia Skoblikova, had the distinction of being the only contestant in the Games to win two individual golds, for the 1500 metres and 3000 metres, setting a new world record in the former. The 500 metres was won by Helga Haase, of Germany, and the 1000 by Klara Guseva, of USSR.

In the men's figure skating at the architectural prize-winning Blyth Arena, American David Jenkins included high triple and double jumps of a standard which no European could match, overhauling a lead in the figures by the Czech, Carol Divin. Jenkins's compatriot and future sister-in-law, Carol Heiss, won the women's event by a comfortable margin and the Canadian combination, Robert Paul and Barbara Wagner, were equally convincing in the pairs.

The United States clinched the ice hockey issue with a 2–1 upset of the form favourites, Canada. It was the first USA win over Canada in any major international ice hockey competition since 1956 and only the third since 1920. The Canadians also defeated the Russians 8–5. The Soviet side suffered a clear setback after their 1956 triumph.

Innsbruck, 1964

The dominant individual in these Games was the Russian speed skater, Lidia Skoblikova, the first competitor ever to win four gold medals at one Winter Olympics. It was not this alone, but the fact that three of her four times were new Olympic records – and all in the space of four days – which caused this 24-year-old blonde Soviet flyer to be the greatest woman ice racer.

Two more Olympic ice speed records were shattered by the men. An American barber, Richard McDermott, shaved a tenth of a second off the old 500-metre time, a full half-second ahead of three who tied for second place, including the respected Russian sprinter, Eugeni Grishin. The other speed record was set by the veteran Norwegian, Knut Johannesen, over 5000 metres.

Queen Juliana of the Netherlands saw an inspired Sjoukje Dijkstra capture her country's first Olympic gold medal in any sport since Fanny Blankers-Koen's athletics triumph in 1948. For technical merit, six of the nine judges gave the powerful Dutch figure skater 5·9 marks out of a possible 6. Manfred Schnelldorfer took the men's title for Germany after seeing his French rival, Alain Calmat, twice fall heavily.

In the pairs event, the classically smooth Russian partnership, Oleg Protopopov and Ludmila Belousova, pipped the German world-title holders, Hans Bäumler and Marika Kilius, in a thrillingly close tussle between the two best pairs to be seen for many years. Protopopov's strength in lifts and his partner's acute-angled edges were rare sights for the connoisseur.

Although the final table suggested that USSR won the ice hockey with plenty to spare, in fact the title was decided by a 3-2 defeat of Canada in their final game. Had the Canadians won that match, the two nations would have finished equal on points, in which case by Olympic rules the victorious team in the match between the two would have been champions.

But there is no question that victory was well merited by the only team to win all seven of its matches and the one with the most goals for and the least against. Keys to the Soviet success were superb fitness, which made them dominant in the final period of every match; superior skating skill, which gave them quicker manoeuvrability; and their forwards' technique of keeping possession until the right scoring chance came.

Grenoble, 1968

There was a shock form upset in one of the figure skating events when Emmerich Danzer, then world men's champion, lapsed in the figures and his fellow Austrian, Wolfgang Schwarz, long accustomed to being Danzer's 'shadow', took the title with dominant free-skating highlighted by well-timed triple salchow, double axel and double flip jumps. American Tim Wood was an ominous runner-up above the Frenchman, Patrick Pera, with Danzer humbled in fourth spot.

A feature of the women's free-skating was the contrasting technique of the classical, frail-looking Peggy Fleming, the United States winner, and the robust East German, Gabriele Seyfert, who came second. The outcome was never in doubt because of the American's substantial lead in the figures. Miss Fleming's slender frame belied a remarkable stamina which sustained a widely varied repertoire of smoothly landed double jumps and gracefully fast spins.

The retention of the pairs title by the Soviet husband-and-wife partnership, Oleg Protopopov and Ludmila Belousova (under which name she always skated), was a commendable achievement at the ages of 35 and 32 respectively. But a long and successful career was obviously nearing its end and many a moist eye breathlessly admired their skilfully timed split lutz lift and characteristic one-handed death spiral.

The speed skating contributed a liberal quantity of thrills, heightened by a cup-tie atmosphere with Dutch and Norwegian supporters armed with rosettes, banners, motor horns and bells. Experts were confounded after predicting that the Grenoble outdoor speed skating oval would not provide such a fast surface as rinks at higher altitudes.

A new world time by the Norwegian, Anton Maier, was set in the men's 5000 metres and, during the eight events, no fewer than 52 improvements were made on existing Olympic records. An important contributory factor may have been the ideally moist ice which had been chemically softened and demineralized to match that formed naturally at mountain rinks.

The Swede, Johnny Höglin, beat Maier by 1·2 seconds to win the 10000 metres. Kees Verkerk defeated his fellow Dutchman, Ard Schenk, in the 1500 metres and Erhard Keller, of West Germany, took the 500-metre sprint.

The Netherlands' high reputation in women's ice racing was upheld by Johanna Schut and Carolina Geijssen, who won the 3000 metres and 1000 metres respectively, but their much-fancied compatriot, Stien Kaiser, only managed two bronze medals after apparently reaching peak form too early.

Ludmila Titova, who won the 500 metres and came second in the 1000 metres, was the only successful Russian competitor in a sport for which Soviet racers had been previously renowned. Three silver medals in one event by competitors from the same nation was an unprecedented occurrence, involving a US trio, Jenny Fish, Dianne Holum and Mary Meyers, in the 500 metres. Although not among the medallists, Patricia Tipper became the first woman to represent Britain in Olympic speed skating.

The Russian stickhandlers began the major eight-team ice hockey contest in unbeatable fashion, outclassing Finland 8–0 and East Germany 9–0, but when Sweden only lost 2–3 to them the outcome suddenly appeared less of a foregone conclusion.

In the outstanding match of the series, the Czechs beat USSR 5–4 in a tense end-to-end affair which kept the excited spectators in suspense. Had Czechoslovakia not been held by Sweden to a 2–2 draw in the penultimate match, the Czechs would have won this tournament through being level on points with USSR, in which case the result of the match between the two, and not goal average, would have decided the issue. So the Russians did not win so comfortably as many had at first anticipated. The title was taken with 12 points from seven games, followed by Czechoslovakia with 11 and Canada 10.

Sapporo, 1972

The motor horns of Dutch fans joyfully greeted the achievements of hero Ard Schenk, the tall, huskily handsome Flying Dutchman who won a hat-trick of gold medals in the men's speed skating; but they were dramatically silenced by a couple of American girls who beat their best in two of the four women's events.

Schenk proved the outstanding ice racer of his age. His long, smooth stride, fast cornering and stylish economy of energy brought him gold medals in the 1500, 5000 and 10000 metres – shattering two Olympic records in the process. His countrymen, Kees Verkerk and Jan Bols, helped underline Dutch supremacy in the men's events except for the more specialized 500-metre sprint, when Erhard Keller, after two false starts, successfully defended his title for West Germany.

Two United States girls, Dianne Holum and Anne Henning, beat the Dutch best in the 1500 metres and 500 metres respectively. Miss Henning, aged 16, became the youngest victor at Sapporo in sensational style. Accidentally baulked by Canadian opponent Sylvia Burka halfway through the heat, she completed the run in Olympic record time and then, accepting her option under the rules to have a second run after all her rivals had finished, skated alone to a new record.

There was a further shock for the Dutch when the West German Monika Pflug won the 1000 metres, but the 'veteran' 33-

year-old Stien Baas-Kaiser finally restored national pride with victory in the 3000 metres.

Ondrej Nepela, who had been the youngest competitor at Innsbruck in 1964, became the first Czech to win an Olympic figure skating title. Exemplary in figures, but less impressive in free-skating, he landed a superb triple salchow jump but fell for the first time in four years when attempting a triple toe loop jump. Sergei Chetverukhin's second place was the highest a Russian had achieved in international solo figure skating.

Some of the best figures ever traced clinched the women's crown for the tall Austrian, Trixi Schuba, whose free-skating was relatively moderate yet adequate for overall victory. There was an enthralling tussle for the silver between two great free-skaters, Canadian Karen Magnussen and American Janet Lynn, who lost the verdict but, despite a fall, got a controversial maximum six for artistic impression.

The closest all-Russian finish came in the pairs, when Moscow's Alexsei Ulanov and Irina Rodnina gained a 6–3 judges' decision over their Leningrad rivals, Andrei Suraikin and Ludmila Smirnova.

The first Winter Olympics to be held in Asia saw the most open ice hockey tournament since Britain's narrow victory of 1936. A 3–3 draw between Sweden and the USSR, followed by a shock 5–1 US win against the Czechs, kept the issue in delicate balance to the final match, when the Russians settled the issue with a 5–2 victory over the Czechs.

It was the third successive Soviet title but their least impressive. The youngest-ever US team gained an unexpected silver medal at Czechoslovakia's expense, thanks largely to the American goalminder, Mike Curran. For the first time Canada, the winner of most Olympic ice hockey titles, did not compete because of an unresolved wrangle concerning professionalism.

Note: Acknowledgment is due to the publishers of my previous books and articles for repeating some of the factual and historical details best left unaltered. Readers interested in the ice and snow sports not on skates will find the Olympic stories of Alpine and Nordic skiing, bobsledding and tobogganing recounted in my *International Encyclopaedia of Winter Sports.*

Olympic Figure Skating Competitions

Men

	Gold	Silver	Bronze
1908 London	Ulrich Salchow (Sweden)	Richard Johansson (Sweden)	Per Thorén (Sweden)
1920 Antwerp	Gillis Grafström (Sweden)	Andreas Krogh (Norway)	Martin Stixrud (Norway)
1924 Chamonix	Gillis Grafström (Sweden)	Willy Böckl (Austria)	Georg Gautschi (Switzerland)
1928 St Moritz	Gillis Grafström (Sweden)	Willy Böckl (Austria)	Bobby van Zeebroeck (Belgium)
1932 Lake Placid	Karl Schäfer (Austria)	Gillis Grafström (Sweden)	Montgomery Wilson (Canada)
1936 Garmisch	Karl Schäfer (Austria)	Ernst Baier (Germany)	Felix Kaspar (Austria)
1948 St Moritz	Dick Button (USA)	Hans Gerschwiler (Switzerland)	Edi Rada (Austria)
1952 Oslo	Dick Button (USA)	Helmut Seibt (Austria)	James Grogan (USA)
1956 Cortina	Hayes Jenkins (USA)	Ronald Robertson (USA)	David Jenkins (USA)
1960 Squaw Valley	David Jenkins (USA)	Carol Divin (Czechoslovakia)	Donald Jackson (Canada)
1964 Innsbruck	Manfred Schnelldorfer (Germany)	Alain Calmat (France)	Scott Allen (USA)
1968 Grenoble	Wolfgang Schwarz (Austria)	Tim Wood (USA)	Patrick Pera (France)
1972 Sapporo	Ondrej Nepela (Czechoslovakia)	Sergei Chetverukhin (USSR)	Patrick Pera (France)

Women

	Gold	Silver	Bronze
1908 London	Madge Syers (Great Britain)	Elsa Rendschmidt (Germany)	Dorothy Greenhough (Great Britain)
1920 Antwerp	Magda Julin-Mauroy (Sweden)	Svea Norén (Sweden)	Theresa Weld (USA)
1924 Chamonix	Herma Plank-Szabo (Austria)	Beatrix Loughran (USA)	Ethel Muckelt (Great Britain)

	Gold	Silver	Bronze
1928 St Moritz	Sonja Henie (Norway)	Fritzi Burger (Austria)	Beatrix Loughran (USA)
1932 Lake Placid	Sonja Henie (Norway)	Fritzi Burger (Austria)	Maribel Vinson (USA)
1936 Garmisch	Sonja Henie (Norway)	Cecilia Colledge (Great Britain)	Vivi-Anne Hultén (Sweden)
1948 St Moritz	Barbara Ann Scott (Canada)	Eva Pawlik (Austria)	Jeannette Altwegg (Great Britain)
1952 Oslo	Jeannette Altwegg (Great Britain)	Tenley Albright (USA)	Jacqueline du Bief (France)
1956 Cortina	Tenley Albright (USA)	Carol Heiss (USA)	Ingrid Wendl (Austria)
1960 Squaw Valley	Carol Heiss (USA)	Sjoukje Dijkstra (Netherlands)	Barbara Roles (USA)
1964 Innsbruck	Sjoukje Dijkstra (Netherlands)	Regine Heitzer (Austria)	Petra Burka (Canada)
1968 Grenoble	Peggy Fleming (USA)	Gabriele Seyfert (East Germany)	Hana Maskova (Czechoslovakia)
1972 Sapporo	Beatrix Schuba (Austria)	Karen Magnussen (Canada)	Janet Lynn (USA)

Pairs

	Gold	Silver	Bronze
1908 London	Heinrich Burger Anna Hübler (Germany)	James Johnson Phyllis Johnson (Great Britain)	Edgar Syers Madge Syers (Great Britain)
1920 Antwerp	Walter Jakobsson Ludowika Eilers (Finland)	Yngvar Bryn Alexia Schöyen (Norway)	Basil Williams Phyllis Johnson (Great Britain)
1924 Chamonix	Alfred Berger Helene Engelmann (Austria)	Walter Jakobsson Ludowika Eilers (Finland)	Pierre Brunet Andrée Joly (France)
1928 St Moritz	Pierre Brunet Andrée Joly (France)	Otto Kaiser Lilly Scholz (Austria)	Ludwig Wrede Melitta Brunner (Austria)
1932 Lake Placid	Pierre Brunet Andrée Joly (France)	Sherwin Badger Beatrix Loughran (USA)	László Szollás Emilie Rotter (Hungary)

	Gold	Silver	Bronze
1936 Garmisch	Ernst Baier Maxie Herber (Germany)	Erich Pausin Ilse Pausin (Austria)	László Szollás Emilie Rotter (Hungary)
1948 St Moritz	Pierre Baugniet Micheline Lannoy (Belgium)	Ede Király Andrea Kékesy (Hungary)	Wallace Distelmeyer Suzanne Morrow (Canada)
1952 Oslo	Paul Falk Ria Baran (Germany)	Peter Kennedy Karol Kennedy (USA)	Laszlo Nagy Marianne Nagy (Hungary)
1956 Cortina	Kurt Oppelt Sissy Schwarz (Austria)	Norris Bowden Frances Dafoe (Canada)	Laszlo Nagy Marianne Nagy (Hungary)
1960 Squaw Valley	Robert Paul Barbara Wagner (Canada)	Hans Bäumler Marika Kilius (Germany)	Ronald Ludington Nancy Ludington (USA)
1964 Innsbruck	Oleg Protopopov Ludmila Belousova (USSR)	Hans Bäumler Marika Kilius (Germany)	Guy Revell Debbi Wilkes (Canada)
1968 Grenoble	Oleg Protopopov Ludmila Belousova (USSR)	Alexandr Gorelik Tatjana Zhuk (USSR)	Wolfgang Danne Margot Glockshuber (West Germany)
1972 Sapporo	Alexsei Ulanov Irina Rodnina (USSR)	Andrei Suraikin Ludmila Smirnova (USSR)	Uwe Kagelmann Manuela Gross (East Germany)

Men's Olympic Ice Speed Skating Competitions

	500 metres	*Time*	*1500 metres*	*Time*
1924 Chamonix	Charles Jewtraw (USA)	44·0	Clas Thunberg (Finland)	2:20·8
1928 St Moritz	Clas Thunberg (Finland)	43·4	Clas Thunberg (Finland)	2:21·1
	Bernt Evensen (Norway)	43·4		
1932 Lake Placid	Jack Shea (USA)	43·4	Jack Shea (USA)	2:57·5
1936 Garmisch	Ivar Ballangrud (Norway)	43·4	Charles Mathiesen (Norway)	2:19·2
1948 St Moritz	Finn Helgesen (Norway)	43·1	Sverre Farstad (Norway)	2:17·6
1952 Oslo	Ken Henry (USA)	43·2	Hjalmar Andersen (Norway)	2:20·4
1956 Cortina	Eugeni Grishin (USSR)	40·2	Eugeni Grishin (USSR)	2:08·6
			Juri Michhailov (USSR)	2:08·6
1960 Squaw Valley	Eugeni Grishin (USSR)	40·2	Roald Aas (Norway)	2:10·4
			Eugeni Grishin (USSR)	2:10·4
1964 Innsbruck	Richard McDermott (USA)	40·1	Ants Antson (USSR)	2:10·3
1968 Grenoble	Erhard Keller (West Germany)	40·3	Kees Verkerk (Netherlands)	2:03·4
1972 Sapporo	Erhard Keller (West Germany)	39·44	Ard Schenk (Netherlands)	2:02·96

Women's Olympic Ice Speed Skating Competitions

	500 metres	*Time*	*1000 metres*	*Time*
1960 Squaw Valley	Helga Haase (Germany)	45·9	Klara Guseva (USSR)	1:34·1

5000 metres	Time	10 000 metres	Time
Clas Thunberg (Finland)	8:39·0	Julius Skutnabb (Finland)	18:04·8
Ivar Ballangrud (Norway)	8:50·5		
Irving Jaffee (USA)	9:40·8	Irving Jaffee (USA)	19:13·6
Ivar Ballangrud (Norway)	8:19·6	Ivar Ballangrud (Norway)	17:24·3
Reidar Liaklev (Norway)	8:29·4	Ake Seyffarth (Sweden)	17:26·3
Hjalmar Andersen (Norway)	8:10·6	Hjalmar Andersen (Norway)	16:45·8
Boris Schilkov (USSR)	7:48·7	Sigvard Ericsson (Sweden	16:35·9
Viktor Kosichkin (USSR)	7:51·3	Knut Johannesen (Norway)	15:46·6
Knut Johannesen (Norway)	7:38·4	Jonny Nilsson (Sweden)	15:50·1
Anton Maier (Norway)	7:22·4	Jonny Höglin (Sweden)	15:23·6
Ard Schenk (Netherlands)	7:23·61	Ard Schenk (Netherlands)	15:01·35

1500 metres	Time	3000 metres	Time
Lidia Skoblikova (USSR)	2:25·2	Lidia Skoblikova (USSR)	5:14·3

	500 metres	*Time*	*1000 metres*	*Time*
1964 Innsbruck	Lidia Skoblikova (USSR)	45·0	Lidia Skoblikova (USSR)	1:33·2
1968 Grenoble	Ludmila Titova (USSR)	46·1	Carolina Geijssen (Netherlands)	1:32·6
1972 Sapporo	Anne Henning (USA)	43·33	Monika Pflug (West Germany)	1:31·40

1500	*Time*	*3000 metres*	*Time*
Lidia Skoblikova (USSR)	2:22·6	Lidia Skoblikova (USSR)	5:14·9
Kaijo Mustonen (Finland)	2:22·4	Ans Schut (Netherlands)	4:56·2
Dianne Holum (USA)	2:20·85	Stien Baas-Kaiser (Netherlands)	4:52·14

L

Olympic Ice Hockey Competitions

	Gold	Silver	Bronze
1920 Antwerp	Canada	USA	Czechoslovakia
1924 Chamonix	Canada	USA	Great Britain
1928 St Moritz	Canada	Sweden	Switzerland
1932 Lake Placid	Canada	USA	Germany
1936 Garmisch	Great Britain	Canada	USA
1948 St Moritz	Canada	Czechoslovakia	Switzerland
1952 Oslo	Canada	USA	Sweden
1956 Cortina	USSR	USA	Canada
1960 Squaw Valley	USA	Canada	USSR
1964 Innsbruck	USSR	Sweden	Czechoslovakia
1968 Grenoble	USSR	Czechoslovakia	Canada
1972 Sapporo	USSR	USA	Czechoslovakia

23. Professional Ice Shows

You do not need a high degree of technical skating ability to join the cast of an ice show. Good appearance and a flair for artistic presentation are just as important and, if you possess the right potential, the major ice-show companies have technical and artistic directors to adapt and improve your ability to suit their requirements. There are good opportunities to travel overseas.

Many stage-struck skaters nowadays join a big touring professional ice show – and are thus paid to do what they most enjoy while seeing life in many lands from a glamorous vantage-point. Interested readers with suitable qualifications should note that vacancies for skaters often exist at any time while the tours are in progress because the right kind are still more rare than one might imagine.

Any girl skater around 5 ft 6 in tall will have the least difficulty in being accepted, but if one is 5 ft 2 in and suited in other requirements, the chances are still good. Boys should be at least 5 ft 8 in tall.

Line skaters normally sign a two-year contract, which usually can be renewed for an extended period. Their basic pay can be appreciably higher than the average income of a well-paid secretary. For many this can be virtually tax-free at home while employed abroad – and what little tax that has to be deducted to meet other countries' legal requirements is of small concern.

All travel costs during the tour, whether by rail, air or sea, are paid by the company – and the fare equivalent is allowed to those who prefer travelling in their own cars, as several do. All this for seeing the world while pursuing one's favourite sport certainly seems a pretty good way of life!

The considerable impact of theatrical skating on the entertainment world was really born in Germany and not in America or Britain, as many might assume. In 1908 a resident ice ballet company was created by Leo Bartuschek at the Berlin Eis Palast. As a result, the first sizeable theatrical skating production was presented at the Admiral Palast, Berlin, in the summer of 1913. It was a style of musical comedy, titled *Flirting at St Moritz*. Stanley Fryett, who later became rink manager at Dundee, Scotland, was an instructor at the Admiral Palast at the time of this show and he told me that it was well worthy of its historic importance and that there were more than a hundred performers in the original Berlin cast. The star was a Berlin girl, Charlotte Oelschlagel.

Meanwhile, in the United States the idea of small ice rinks for skating cabarets in the dining-rooms of leading hotels was introduced in 1914 by Frank Bearing with remarkable success at the Sherman Hotel in Chicago. Other hotels quickly followed suit and in 1915 the great popularity of this new vogue encouraged Charles Dillingham, director of the New York Hippodrome, to import the German production from the Admiral Palast. The entire surface of the great American playhouse stage – 45 feet by 90 feet – was frozen for the original spectacle, *Flirting at St Moritz*. It was the beginning of real fame for Charlotte, whose surname became quickly forgotten, but never her skating, for Charlotte was enthusiastically acclaimed and in 1915 became the first skating film star in a six-episode serial called *The Frozen Warning*.

In 1917, interest in show skating was unabated and the Waldorf-Astoria Hotel in New York installed a rink. The years of the First World War hindered progress, of course, particularly in Europe, and it was consequently not until 1926 that skating was first presented in an English theatre – a production called *Ballets on Ice*, on the stage of the London Coliseum. This was followed by an ice presentation at the London Stoll (where the Royalty now stands) in 1930.

In 1932, Bournemouth's Westover ice rink, British pioneer of annual ice shows, introduced its first musical skating comedy,

Arabian Nights, starring Phil Taylor. In 1936 Claude Langdon presented his first ice show, *Marina,* at Brighton, restaging it the next year at Blackpool and in 1938 at London's Empress Hall.

In 1937, London's first major ice ballet was appropriately performed on a specially built tank at the Royal Opera House, Covent Garden. The hundred-strong cast included Belita, then aged 14, Phil Taylor and the former world pair champions, Pierre Brunet and Andrée Joly. The following year, the London Coliseum presented *St Moritz,* a spectacle which excited impresarios by clearly revealing the potentialities of ice in the theatre, but the progress thus stimulated was destined to be put on ice, in a sadly different sense, until after the Second World War.

While all this was happening in England, that little girl from Oslo who had first startled everyone by appearing in the 1924 Winter Olympics at the age of 11, turned professional in 1936 with ten world, ten European and three Olympic titles to her credit. It must have been getting monotonous.

That May, wittingly or not, Sonja Henie did more to promote the popularity and awareness of skating than any one person ever had before, with her starring role in the first full-length skating feature film, a simple, romantic story called *One in a Million.* It won so very many hearts and brought skating – as no other medium then could – into the minds of multitudes of cinemagoers throughout the world.

To the younger readers I implore, when next this film is re-shown on television, *do* see it because, even allowing for the technical shortcomings of its time, you will not regret it. Films Sonja has starred in since include *Thin Ice, Happy Landing, My Lucky Star, Second Fiddle, Everything Happens at Night, Sun Valley Serenade, Iceland, Wintertime, It's a Pleasure, Countess of Monte Cristo* and *Hullo London.* Together, they are an important part of skating's history.

Oscar Johnson, Eddie Shipstad and Roy Shipstad launched America's first big-scale touring skating revue, *Ice Follies,* at Tulsa, Oklahoma, in 1936. From this modest beginning, with a cast of just twenty-three skaters, *Ice Follies* soon moved from strength to strength and its annual year-long tours have brought fame to many skating-show artistes.

Soon after *Ice Follies* began, Sonja Henie joined with Arthur M. Wirtz to inaugurate a rival touring show called *Hollywood Ice Revue*. The same team installed a rink on the stage of New York's Center Theatre in 1940 and ran ice shows there for ten years. Another New York stage, the Roxy Theatre, was fitted with an ice rink in 1948, when Barbara Ann Scott was its first star.

In 1940 John H. Harris began his annual *Ice Capades* tours. Four years later Emery Gilbert, soon to be joined by Morris Chalfen and George Tyson, started his *Holiday on Ice* series. By using its own portable rink equipment, *Holiday on Ice* was the first of the big companies to present ice spectacles in rinkless areas and, from 1950, extended its field of operations throughout the world.

Meanwhile in Britain, Blackpool Ice Drome was built in 1937 and designed primarily for ice shows. Annual summer editions of Leonard Thompson's *Ice Parade* have been staged there since 1940. But it was theatre magnate Tom Arnold who really sparked off Britain's big post-war revival with *Hot Ice* at Brighton in 1945. The following year, he transformed London's Stoll Theatre into a regular ice theatre, with Cecilia Colledge its first star. These were the first ice shows to be produced by Gerald Palmer, who went on to mastermind a record 130 in Britain, Europe, South Africa and Australia.

Britain was the first country to present ice shows with a story continuity, as distinct from revue, and transposition of the uniquely British traditional Christmas theatre pantomime was an obvious beginning. For the record, the first sizeable ice panto-mime was performed at Purley, on the southern outskirts of London, in 1933. But the first performances of this kind to be staged in the 'grand manner' were Claude Langdon's *Cinderella* at London's Empress Hall and Tom Arnold's *Aladdin* at Brighton, both in 1949.

History was made in the summer of 1950 at London's Harringay Arena, where the first full-length stage musical ever to be presented on ice, *Rose Marie* – the first ice operetta, in fact – starred Barbara Ann Scott and Michael Kirby, with Gerald Palmer producing.

In those early post-war boom years, big money lured the kind of music-hall acts who today would be dubbed 'superstars'. The skate-mindedness of London theatregoers in those money-spinning times was so pronounced that there may well have been a true-life foundation for the story of the woman who stopped outside the Earls Court Motor Show to ask: 'Is it on ice?'

Wembley's first ice pantomime, *Dick Whittington* in 1950, heralded that famous rink's since unbroken era of lavish, expensive skating spectacles, all produced by Palmer, with a resplendent wealth of costumes and décor setting a new precedent in any form of show business, the like of which a conventional theatre's budget could not match. One of Wembley's best ice presentations, *Chu Chin Chow* in 1953, was honoured by the choice of its star, Gloria Nord, to appear before the Queen in a special skating sequence in that year's Royal Variety at the London Coliseum. *White Horse Inn*, at Empress Hall, Ivor Novello's *Perchance to Dream* and Walt Disney's *Snow White and the Seven Dwarfs*, both at Wembley, have been other particularly successful musicals adapted to ice. All have had dialogues dubbed by off-ice voices and mimed by the skaters.

The big American-owned constantly touring revues, *Holiday on Ice*, *Ice Follies* and *Ice Capades*, continue to thrive with a basic revue format in best Holywood-style tradition, specializing in production numbers from famous musical shows, and including in their casts many ex-amateur world champions.

When narrating a more detailed history of ice shows in an earlier book, *This Skating Age* (Stanley Paul, 1958), I wrote:

Will skating shows remain such a popular form of entertainment? Is it possible to continue putting on these lavish presentations indefinitely? So long as promoters with sufficient resources have producers of wide vision and experience with a host of technical experts gathered round them, I can see no reason why these shows should not become as lasting a form of entertainment as ballet or opera. One day we shall see an entire show devoted to a story superbly and clearly enacted on skates without any dialogue at all. We shall also watch these frozen assets broadcast direct from special television ice studios.

These views are still firmly held. The prediction about a story without words has yet to be realized, but, of course, lavish television ice specials have proved extremely popular, notably including such skaters as Peggy Fleming, Karen Magnussen and Janet Lynn. In Sweden, at the palatial Scandinavium arena in Gothenburg, colourfully costumed amateur children's shows by 250 'Scandinavium Ice Kids' are now being ambitiously produced by Maj-Britt, the former Swedish theatrical skater, whose choreographic ability is nearing the goal of self-explanatory mime to eliminate the need for dialogue or narration.

To aim for the very top in professional ice shows, one would have to start very young and devote all spare time not only to figure skating, but to ballet also. To become a minor principal, novel speciality act or member of the *corps de ballet*, however, it is not essential to be so technically talented; but I strongly advocate a study of ballet in addition to skating, in order to improve particularly the gracefulness of arm and hand movements and, in general, personality appeal.

If you have a natural flair for show skating, let me reassure you – in case you are thinking it is too difficult – that it is possible to become a chorus girl or boy after only a year or so of skating and even without having taken a skating test at all. There are many who have started a successful career in this way, improving while they have been earning, and, as has been said, a chorine's pay compares favourably with that of a secretary.

Whether you skate for pleasure or profit, make no mistake about one thing – it's going to be great fun and you will surely be in the fashion of tomorrow.

Index

Compiled by the author